Bridge:
Light Up Your
Understanding of
Bidding

William J. August

Rutledge Books ❖ Bethel, CT

Copyright © 1995 by William J. August
All rights reserved.
Manufactured in the United States of America
ISBN 0-9643937-0-0

Library of Congress Cataloging-in-Publication Data

August, William J.
    Bridge : light up your understanding
of bidding / William J. August.
        p. cm.
    ISBN 0-9643937-0-0
    1. Contract bridge—Bidding. I. Title.
GV1282.4   95-69001
795.4152—dc20   CIP

Acknowledgements

This book is dedicated to many great people, some who happen to be great bridge personalities. The first group are some who are now playing at a bridge table in heaven who were friends, partners, confidants, teachers, and advisers.

They are Jack Kushner, Larry Weiss, Harold Ogust, Jim Jacoby, Dick Frey, Sam Stayman, Charles Goren, B. Jay Becker, and Easley Blackwood.

The second group is the Bridge Teachers of America. We need you!

I sincerely and deeply thank all of my friends who have helped, but in particular Eddie Kantar, Bill Root, Benito Garozzo, and Billy Eisenberg for allowing me to pick their brains regarding theory and ideas over the years.

Special thanks must be given to Gerry Cohn, a friend and very special man who in his quiet way influenced me to finish the book and to Sidney Jacobson and Arthur Meyer who said, "Get it done and it will be good."

The suggestions and support of friends Mimi and Maury Bronner, Louisa and Rufus Finch, and Jeanni and Gerry Levy are most appreciated. Thanks also to Larry Martin and Steve Barcus, my main sounding boards. Thanks as well to Ken Karlan for putting things together and to the staff at Rutledge Books, and very special thanks to Gloria for living with a bridge "nut" and putting up with me and my computer.

The next page is a letter to you, the reader of this book.

Dear Friend,

I love bridge! It is truly a great game and a greater pasttime. Everyone should play it. However, some players actually drive others away from the game. I apologize for those whose method of play, approach to the game, and unacceptable demeanor cause many others to stay away from bridge. Certain lawsuits prevent me from listing some of their names.

However, there are many great ladies and gentlemen who play the game, have fun, and make all new players feel relaxed and welcome to the bridge world. No writer of any bridge book has ever dedicated even a page to them. Now is the time!

I wish to acknowledge some of those whom I have played with and against in my former playing days, and who have done everything wonderful to attract new players to the game. Nobody acknowledges them as they should be but they are the true reasons for playing the game. They are:

Edgar Kaplan, Dorothy Hayden Truscott, Bob Hammon, Marshall Miles, Bobby Wolff, Howard Perlman, Tom Smith, Alfred Sheinwold, Bill Seamon, Amalya Kearse, Steve Altman, Richard Goldberg, Gary Hayden, and Russ Arnold.

How about Edith Kemp Freilich, Steve and Michael Becker, Boris Koytchou, Frank Stewart, Zeke Jabbour, Paul Soloway, Gaylor Kasle, Mark Blumenthal, Gail Greenberg, Jeff Rubens, Carol and Tom Sanders, Joyce and Harold Lilie, Tannah Hirsch, Judy and Norman Kay, Robert Rosen, Allan Falk, Dan Rotman, Henry Francis, Laura Jane Gordy, Matt Granovetter, Nancy Gruver, and Jo Morse. And I must mention Antha Mallander, Leonard Harmon, Tim Holland, Eric Kokish, Don Krauss, Lou and Gloria Levy, Dennis McGarry, Vic Mitchell, Dan Morse, Neil Silverman, Sandy and Roger Stern, Sandy and Paul Trent, Alan Truscott, Ron Von Der Porten, and Kathy Wei-Sender.

There are others whoses names have been omitted without intent. If you read this and promote the game with selfless motivation, consider your name mentioned.

Thanks to you all,

Bill August

Bridge: Light Up Your Understanding of Bidding

Contents

Foreword

This book is an effort to reach you intellectually. After all, bridge is a game in which intellect is very important. The proper use of your thinking and reasoning power will allow you to reach a complete understanding of the game. After all, logic and reason constitute the basis of the game of bridge.

It is difficult, perhaps impossible, to evaluate one's personal bridge skills. Think about your skills relative to those of the top players. If you are the best player in a very poor group, you still may be a poor player. In the average bridge game, somebody always emerges as the "authority" telling everyone else what was done wrong and/or what should have been done. Since you have been in that position more than once, this is your opportunity to really understand the bidding portion of the game. Reaching the correct contract is mandatory so put your ego aside and allow me to help you become a higher-quality player.

Anyone with desire can become a solid player by understanding, mastering, and then applying basic concepts. If your efforts to learn are pooh-poohed, look carefully at your critics. Ask what qualifications they possess which allows them to judge your efforts. If a critic justifies his opinion with, "I've been playing for twenty years and I should know," then you know that he knows very little. If he says that he "took lessons from so-and-so," it means nothing. Any qualified teacher would have to agree with the concepts to which you will be exposed.

An example (of which there are many) which illustrates the lack of conceptual knowledge is offered here. Bridge is a game of logic! Bridge is a game of reason! Bridge Bidding is a game of "SHOW AND TELL"! Bridge is a game of messages! With this hand as dealer, ♠9 ♥AKJ9 ♦97642 ♣A98, too many modern players would either Pass or open the bidding with one diamond. The first group would argue that they have *only* 12 points because they were told <u>not</u> to count length values until a suit is agreed upon. The second group would argue that they cannot open one heart because they have *only* four cards in that suit. Absurd!

Today, most players incorporate into their bidding structure a method which is called "five-card majors". The "creme de la creme," when the **TIME IS RIGHT,** will open a major suit even though there are only **FOUR CARDS** in it. Can you imagine that? Perhaps *you* should wonder why some of the finest players occasionally open the bidding with a four-card major. The answer is part of a concept and is in this text *for your eyes only.*

THIS BOOK IS FOR YOU—Enjoy it!

"BID TO THE CORRECT CONTRACT AND KNOW
YOUR PARTNER'S HAND"

CHAPTER ONE

AN EXPLANATION OF SORTS

More than eleven million persons play bridge in America, and all of them are addicted to the idea of playing better and playing with better partners. Many of them play as often as five times a week and a large percentage play at least three times a week. Regardless of how often you play or whether you are a novice, an intermediate, or an advanced player, this book is for you.

The learning process of this wonderful and exhilarating game called bridge can be made unnecessarily and perplexingly complex, or it can be as simple as A B C. Bridge is a game of information. Many ask why it is so difficult to learn to play well. The answer: very few players have mastered the basic concepts. Players don't know why a certain bid must be made and why another bid may be incorrect. If a player opens the bidding 1♣, an overwhelming majority of players automatically think that *partner probably doesn't have clubs*. This ridiculous conclusion is just one example of how incorrect thinking makes it difficult for a partnership to become proficient.

Unfortunately, most players do not understand bidding structure and have no idea of how to build bridge ideas.

This is primarily the fault of today's teachers. "Point Count" is a tool used to assist a player in evaluating his potential for developing tricks, yet most players don't understand tricks or trick production. Teachers make little effort to explain that there are only thirteen cards in any suit and only thirteen cards in any hand.

People don't know how to "count a hand" from either the bidding or the play. How many times have you heard that you should open the bidding if you have thirteen points? How many times have you been chided for opening a hand with twelve points? There are many thirteen point hands that should NOT be opened and there are many twelve and even eleven point hands that SHOULD be opened.

A player should learn to evaluate his hand correctly. A bridge partnership should then learn to speak the "language" fluently. A bid should be translated correctly—it should *never* offer different meanings from a player's tongue to his partner's mind. A partnership should attempt to bid naturally in an effort to avoid misunderstandings. It makes little sense to make unnatural bids because unnatural bids often result in misunderstandings. SHOW AND TELL!

Widespread use of conventions has had a crippling effect on the development of basic skills. The use of conventions introduces a myriad of unnatural bids. This necessitates a translation into an intended meaning and then an adjustment of the meaning of the bid to the situation in which it is used. This borders on the bizarre. More than seven hundred different conventions have been devised and VERY FEW can make you a better player. If you are a highly skillful bidder with a high degree of proficiency in the play of the cards, then perhaps the use of certain conventions can make your game a little more fine-tuned. The terrible pitfall in the use of conventions is that the user often does not understand them fully nor does he use them correctly. People are always looking for an excuse to bid, and conventions give them a built-in excuse to bid when in fact no bid should be considered. I know of hundreds, even thousands of players who cannot play their way out of the proverbial "paper bag" who use more conventions and variations than some of the finest players in the world.

♣ ♥ ♠ ♦

It is my unwavering contention that increased expertise will come ever so much faster and with little wasted effort if one learns the basic concepts of bidding.

I believe the material in this text is *invaluable*, not just important. It is a distillation of thoughts from more than thirty years of playing, teaching, writing, and observing. Those who taught and influenced me were some of the greatest theorists and some of the finest players in the world.

Since I am not a "shrinking violet," I never hesitated to call or write to the most knowledgeable people in the bridge world for their ideas on any subject material. I always sought answers in the form of theory or concept. To know "what" to bid with a particular hand was not good enough. I wanted to know "why" a certain bid was made or "why" other bids were rejected. I was amazed by the consistency in reasoning that the true experts of past days offered to back up their answers. The players of today seem to lack consistency in reasoning. Too many scream their answers too loudly as a cover-up for their failure to offer logical reasons for their bidding.

Therefore, this text is a presentation, not of new ideas or radical notions, but of thoughts and theories which are essential to learning the game correctly. Statements are made and the "whys" are explored and given to you in concept form. What you can learn from this document is not what Bill August thinks, but, in principle, what the best minds in bridge generally agree upon regarding basic principles.

Most bridge books seem like science textbooks. They are difficult to understand because few statements are made that are easily explained to the average reader.

Regarding Teaching

When I became reasonably proficient at this wonderful game, I started teaching and found that I had a natural aptitude for conveying the "bridge message" to others. Time, experience and hundreds of thousands of hands played against all systems and all opponents soon brought home the realization that not many players really know much about the game. THIS BOOK IS FOR THEM.

Out of necessity, I commenced writing teaching pamphlets with the common theme of a LOGICAL approach to bridge. This "logical" approach was a successful method of reaching the student and allowed him an unlimited horizon of learning. Meanwhile, I felt an exasperation building within myself with regards to other teachers whose students were learning little about the "game".

I am embarrassed by the great number of people who teach bridge who are completely ill-equipped to do so. I am also embarrassed by those who teach quantity and not quality, and who would fail almost any examination if their knowledge, not their memory, were tested. They use phrases like "second hand low" or "third hand high" without explaining why and in what framework those phrases might be correct. Some say, "always open a hand of thirteen points", yet many hands of that value should not be opened. Others say "never lead from a King", yet many times leading from a King is mandatory. Perhaps it is best to recognize that "always" never exists and "never" never occurs.

Regarding Today's Players

Of the estimated eleven million people who play bridge, fewer than 200,000 belong to the American Contract Bridge

League (ACBL). This organization supervises the business of bridge and conducts tournaments for those who wish to compete. The majority of the better players belong to the ACBL and there might be a few thousand non-affiliated players who play well by League standards. It is assumed that this group (two hundred thousand) represents the cream of the crop. This is about 2% of all players.

Just think! You may be in that group, but it's not a big deal because that 2% must be divided again. Within that last small group, it is estimated that only about four or five thousand top players truly understand the concepts of the game. These "fine" players are the "creme de la creme" and all are CHAMPIONS.

Champions share three things in common. (1) They have a total grasp of basics. (2) They have a skill-level far above everyone else. (3) They have the capacity and discipline to play "within themselves." THIS BOOK IS NOT FOR THEM!

Because of outstanding talent, they can blend various conventions and treatments (new ammunition) into their structure. Yet they are the first to point out that other than the "creme de la creme," players should not stray from a simple bidding structure unless or until they become proficient in execution. This means "stay with the basics until you become a good player."

There is no better example of the philosophy of staying with the basics than the awareness of seeing Jack Nicklaus play golf. One cannot calculate the thousands of hours of practice that made his golf swing simple and smooth. He never tried hooks, fades, draws, bump and runs, and other techniques until long after he learned and mastered the basics. Every member of a Hall Of Fame in any of the arts or sports reached the pinnacle by practicing and perfecting basic skills.

Regarding Fancy Conventions:

When Jane Doe or John Smith sees a fine player using special conventions, it is too often assumed that the fine player became good because of his use of conventions. One might say to partner, "let's play convention 'A' because Mr. X does and he wins." This is a fallacy.

Some partnerships use methods designed solely to take advantage of players of lesser ability. They do things that they would NOT do against top players. Have you ever thought about this? Your manner of coping should be to increase your skill-level so you can perform well against good competition. It matters not at what level you wish to compete—it all starts with the basics.

Some of the finest players make fun of themselves when they botch or forget one of their many conventions or variations. They are aware that disaster lurks behind the use of fancy bids and plays. On balance, their success rate is very high. It is normal and reasonable that your use of "fancy" bids will incur many more errors with greater frequency. So, if you wish to play bridge with a plethora of fancy gadgets, THIS BOOK IS NOT FOR YOU!

This book is a presentation of "ideas" so that you may gain an overview of the game. The ideas become concepts. Thinking people who understand a concept or a notion can usually work things out within a given framework. Bridge players are thinking people. Bridge players learn to "SHOW AND TELL."

These ideas and concepts embrace four segments of bidding starting with the material relative to the OPENING BIDDER as segment number one. The second segment is that which affects his partner, THE RESPONDER to the opening bidder. This will take the reader through chapter four. On the way, you will learn no-trump bidding and opening two-bids, both weak and strong.

The third and fourth segments are devoted to their opponents, also known as DEFENSIVE BIDDERS. Segment three is material relative to the player known as THE OVERCALLER who sits in the second seat, directly to the left of the opening bidder. The final segment is devoted to the player often in the fourth seat called the man in the BALANCING SEAT. He is to the right of the opening bidder. However, in certain auctions the balancing bidder could be in either seat. This material is presented in chapters five through seven.

CHAPTER TWO

BUILDING BLOCKS

No person, whether novice, intermediate or seasoned, can truly become proficient at bridge without a thorough knowledge of what is *supposed* to happen and how to *make things* happen. Becoming proficient usually means becoming **DISCIPLINED!**

Bridge is a game of many concepts. Each is an imaginary link in a long chain. The chain becomes stronger as each link is properly forged and then joined with another. A bridge partnership becomes stronger as both players learn to understand the concepts and then become skillful in their execution. Few players (including those that you know) are proficient because they lack knowledge of basic concepts. Partners must send messages to each other to "describe their hands." Each message is part of SHOW AND TELL. When this is done well, the partnership achieves a level of proficiency that gives enjoyment and offers the thrill of intellectual challenge.

A competent teacher continually emphasizes and repeats pertinent words and phrases in order to condition the reader or listener to basic mechanics and thought-structure. Some of the words and phrases, but not all of them, follow. If you learn them well, it is almost guaranteed that with effort and practice you can learn the language of bridge and start to become a good player.

Thirteen commonly used words, are presented for your benefit.

AUCTION—A bidding process to determine the contract.

BID—An undertaking to win at least a specified number of tricks in a specified denomination.

CALL—Any time a player speaks during an auction (questions and conversations excluded). Every bid is a *call*, but not every *call* is a bid.

CONTRACT—The undertaking by declarer's side to win, at the denomination named, the number of tricks specified in the final bid, whether undoubled, doubled or redoubled.

DECLARER—The person who plays the hand.

DEFENDER—The two opponents of the declarer.

HONOR CARD—Any Ace, King, Queen, Jack or Ten.

LEAD—The first card played to any trick.

OPENING LEAD—The card led on the *first trick*.

PARTNER—That person with whom one plays as a team against the other two players. Try to choose wisely or you may feel that you are playing against three opponents.

PASS—A call specifying that the player (at that turn) does not wish to, or cannot, say something definitive.

TRICK—The unit which determines the outcome of the contract. A trick consists of four cards, one contributed by each player in proper rotation.

TRUMP—Each card in a specified suit named in the final contract.

The three elements of Bridge are bidding, play and defense. In each, there is a common denominator called a TRICK. Bidding is used to estimate the number of tricks the combined hands of a partnership will produce. Play offers an opportunity for declarer to back the partnership judgment by taking those tricks. Defense is when the opponents try to thwart the declarer and cause him to take fewer tricks than were contracted for.

There Are <u>Three</u> Kinds of Tricks That Can Be Won

1. **HIGH-CARD WINNER:** The most apparent and obvious method of winning a trick is through the power of the highest card played on *that given trick*. If, in order, players numbered one, two, three, and four played the...<u>two</u>, <u>seven</u>, <u>King</u>, and <u>Ace</u> in a designated suit, the player who played the Ace would have won the trick by virtue of having played the highest card. Too bad for the man who played the King. Perhaps he thought he was going to win the trick, and he certainly would have if that dastardly scoundrel who played after him did NOT own the Ace.

2. **LONG-CARD WINNER:** This (too often neglected) winner is the salvation of the majority of hands. It is *that* card which, though perhaps relatively small in size, assumes the stature of an Ace by virtue of exhaustion.

"Exhaustion," in a playing sense, means playing a suit as many times as necessary until no one else has any cards in that suit. The remaining card(s) are now winners.

In the following example, if you held the clubs in the South seat, you could lead the King which loses to the Ace. When you recapture the lead in another suit, you could then play the Queen, which is a **high-card winner**. At this point, eight clubs have been played. If you now led your little two-spot, again with everybody following, this trick would lose to the opponent's Jack. The suit is now completely exhausted as you have the thirteenth, and last, club. Do you see that little devil? Well, that three-spot is a **long-card winner** because no one can beat it.

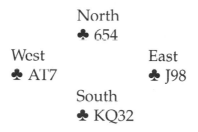

3. TRUMP WINNER: Any card in a specified suit agreed on through the bidding process as "trumps." From this suit, any card can be played to a trick of any <u>other</u> suit in which the player has no cards (a void). A trump can be beaten only by a higher trump and even the smallest trump can negate the **HIGH CARD** power of an Ace in another suit.

There are other phrases and words which must be comprehended in order to play bridge.

SIZE OF HAND—The point-count value in high cards and/or distribution in a given hand. SIZE is usually given in "three-point" spreads.

BRACKET—A term used to describe the three-point spread in which a hand belongs. First bracket = 13–15, second bracket = 16–18, etc. A nice and easy way to describe a hand's SIZE. An easy way to think of partner's hand.

SHAPE OF HAND—The description of any hand which indicates the suit or suits present.

PREFERENCE—It is expected that when a player bids two or more suits (showing shape), partner will <u>prefer</u> one of them. PREFERENCE is determined by the **number of cards** one holds in the two suits. Therefore, when holding *more* cards in the first bid suit, return to that first suit. With equal numbers, do the same.

VOID, SINGLETON, DOUBLETON—the words used to describe any suit in which there are no cards, one card or two cards, respectively.

BIDDING OBJECTIVES—Major suits, No-Trump, and Minor suits. The bidding process is usually directed (provided the partnership meets the requirements) to a final contract in the above order of preference with the MAJOR suits given the highest priority.

MINIMUM OPENING BID—Any opening bid of less than 19 points. The **true minimum** is 13–15 points and the **minimum plus** is 16–18 points. Note the three-point spreads or "brackets"!

MAXIMUM OPENING BID—-Any opening bid of 19 points or more. The **true maximum** is 19–21 points and the *maximum-plus* is 22 points or more. Again, note the three-point spreads.

CHAPTER THREE

THE OPENING BID, INITIAL RESPONSE, & OPENER'S REBID

The opening bid is comprised of three parts. Those who consider themselves to be knowledgeable players will be more proficient if they understand the concept and theory behind this bid.

1. POINT COUNT—It is "accepted" that 13 points is needed to open the bidding with a suit bid of ONE. The points come from HIGH-CARD values (Aces, Kings, Queens and Jacks) and DISTRIBUTIONAL values of "shortness" (voids, singletons and doubletons). Some players give DISTRIBUTIONAL values to suit *length* rather than to "shortness". Both methods are about the same. Does it take a genius to realize that the longer a suit gets, the shorter another suit has to be?

Why is it "accepted" that 13 is the number of points necessary for an opening bid?

Under the ideal circumstance of a perfect deal, each player is entitled to an Ace, a King, a Queen and a Jack (ten high-card points). Each player is also entitled to a "four-card" suit and three "three-card" suits. These entitlements preclude the presence of any distributional points. The combined strength of each partnership is twenty high-card points. When the deal described is evident, the trick-taking potential of each partnership is even and, because the thirteenth trick cannot be cut in half, one partnership will take seven tricks and the other will take six. This is a virtual tie. However, if a King (3 points) were taken from any hand and added to an opponent's hand, one pair's strength would be increased to a combined total of twenty-three points and the other pair's strength would be reduced to a combined total of seventeen points. The differential is such that the pair with the greater strength now has the capacity to increase its trick-taking potential to eight while reducing the opponents to five.

2. DEFENSIVE STRENGTH—$2^1/2$ tricks (when a player becomes more accomplished, two tricks). When one opens the bidding in an effort to become declarer, it doesn't mean he will successfully "buy" the final contract. Quite frequently, one of the opponents will win the bidding war and the right to play the hand. It is because of this possibility that the opening bidder should have, as part of his opening bid, certain cards or combinations of cards that will almost guarantee his taking tricks <u>against the opponents</u>. These are defensive tricks and are also referred to as "quick tricks" or "honor tricks." Examples:

$$AK=2 \quad AQ=1^1/2 \quad KQ=1 \quad A=1 \quad Kx=^1/2$$

Why is it essential that "two-and-a-half defensive tricks" be a part of an opening bid?

There are eight defensive tricks to a deal, two in each suit.

The ideal circumstance would allow each player two tricks which is his fair share. Again, in the perfect deal, the defensive capacity of each partnership is the same—a tie.

The King which was removed from one hand to an opponent's represents a half-trick and ensures one partnership a capacity for taking a greater number of tricks on *defense*. Your partner will expect this opening-bid requirement which will assist his decision-making when the opponents enter the auction after you have opened the bidding.

3. THE SUIT—Any suit chosen as the "vehicle" with which to start the bidding should meet certain minimal requirements. A useful rule of thumb to determine a MINIMUM BIDDABLE SUIT is that if the suit were no more than four cards in length, it should be headed by at least the Queen, Jack and nine. Example: QJ9x. An "x" is the mark used to denote a small card. All five-card suits headed by the Queen or better, and any six-card suit, are good enough with which to open the bidding. <u>This concept must be used whenever the opening bid is ONLY thirteen points!</u>

Why should the suit which is opened meet minimum requirements?

Minimum requirements are established as a "buffer" when opening the bidding with the barest minimum of thirteen points. Often, the suit becomes the eventual trump suit and one should be confident that he can take tricks in that suit. Also, if the opponents should "buy" the hand and partner starts the defense, he should be comfortable in the fact that he can lead "the suit which was opened". As an opening hand becomes greater in strength, the minimum suit requirements become less relevant.

<u>VERY IMPORTANT</u>

The requirements of "point-count," "defensive strength" and "minimum biddable suits" are absolutely essential when building a fundamentally sound game. Every top player knows this. At some point he incorporated this foundation into his game. The strict requirements apply to every hand which is deemed to be absolutely minimum. **Modifications in numbers 2 and 3 are allowed with stronger hands and/or when the players reach a higher level of proficiency.**

Unfortunately, few players are willing or able to accurately evaluate the level of proficiency at which they play. Almost every player thinks he is much better than he actually is. This over-inflation of one's abilities is a major handicap to growth, learning and improvement. To overcome this natural problem and to become a good partner, one must become DISCIPLINED and work very hard to master fundamentals. Why don't you turn back to page 10 and read the first and second paragraphs again?

The Initial Response

The partner of the opener is the only player at the table who is named the "Responder." If he is not interfered with by an opposing player, it is mandated that he bid with as few as six points in his hand. If he responds in a suit, he is allowed to add his distributional points to his high-card points, but if he responds in "no-trump," he is allowed to count high-card points only. The responder should bid in a pattern which is designed to carry both positive and negative messages to the opener. This thought will be more fully developed as we go along. The pattern is referred to as bidding "up the ladder" and is a most important discipline. In order to minimize errors, modifications in the "up the ladder" principle should not be considered until players become proficient. When reading, studying and playing, reference is often made to the Principle Of One-Over-

One. This principle is synonymous with "up the ladder."

This is the ladder which will have greater significance in bidding as the responding concept is developed. It doesn't matter which suit is opened. The Responder should bid "up the ladder" at the one-level with any FOUR-CARD suit he has. If he has more than one FOUR CARD suit, he should bid the first one available going "up the ladder." (An exception to this will be learned later.)

>>DANGER ZONE<<
>>2NT<<

2♠	2♠
2♥	2♥
2♦	2♦
2♣	2♣
1NT	1NT
1♠	1♠
1♥	1♥
1♦	1♦
1♣	1♣

The responder generally transmits more than one message to the opener. A suit response shows at least six points in the hand and four or more cards in that suit. There is no promise that the placement of high cards are in the suit named. The initial response states two positive features: the point-count and the suit length.

Example: Consider an opening bid of 1♣ with a response of 1♦. The responder promised that he held (1) at least six points and (2) at least four diamonds. As an extension of those two positive statements, a most exciting part of bridge takes place. In the next paragraph, the necessity of discipline and of a proper thought-process illustrates *negative* inferences. The ability to draw inferences correctly is needed to play the game well.

IMPORTANT, IMPORTANT, IMPORTANT !!!!

Using "up the ladder" bidding or the Principle Of One-Over-One, and the same opening bid of 1♣, imagine that Responder bid 1♥ instead of 1♦. Again he has "told" partner that he holds at least six points and at least four hearts.

In addition, he has given partner the added information that IF the heart suit is only four cards long, then he *cannot* have as many as four diamonds. Taking this thought a step further, Responder *could* have four diamonds but that would guarantee the heart length to be at least five cards.

Think about it! The concept applies in many ways and as your level of skill increases, more of those ways will surface. The principle involved allows one to learn much about partner's hand by deduction. You will achieve a predictive capability as the result of deductive reasoning. There are "exceptions," of course. A valid argument can be made for bidding 1♥ in response to a 1♣ opener with: ♠72 ♥AKQ8 ♦7642 ♣962. However, there are compelling reasons NOT to bypass the diamond holding.

Regardless of any "exception," the concept must be learned and understood. Whenever an exception to a "guideline" occurs, partner may draw inaccurate conclusions about your hand. It is ONLY because of this possibility that disciplined guidelines should be adhered to. There are exceptions to almost everything in bridge but, at this juncture, understanding concepts and exercising discipline outweigh any justification for using "exceptions."

Logic and Reason

A sincere student of the game might think about what he has just read and he might (hopefully) conclude that the name of this game could well be changed from Bridge to "SHOW AND TELL" or to "Logic and Reason." Furthermore, if bridge thoughts were presented logically, he should be confident of his ability to learn the game well enough to enjoy it. No overwhelming effort is needed to commit certain things to memory.

Without being facetious, it must be stated that understanding what has to be done is easy and the number of concepts to learn is not burdensome. However, in learning bridge, there are two matters which are not simple. First is the subversion of one's ego to the discipline which is needed to become a good partner. Second is the effort one wishes to expend to think logically and reasonably. In general, people trained in the law, and others who have been trained to think in a logical and reasonable manner, tend to become good bridge players. So from this point on, through all your bridge learning, let's allow LOGIC and REASON to be major influences on your game.

Now, dear reader, please pay special attention to the following three definitions, which are <u>UNDERLINED</u>, <u>CAPITALIZED</u>, <u>BOLD-FACED</u> and <u>NUMBERED</u>.

Understanding them fully will allow you to learn the most important facets of the game and will ensure that you have the "BACKBONE" of bridge properly in place. In one form or another, all three will be in evidence in almost every hand.

1. <u>OPENER'S REBID</u>—The most important call in bridge! This is Opener's <u>second</u> bid (his rebid) and is supposed to describe his bracket and shape.

2 . <u>RESPONDER'S REBID</u>—The second most important call in bridge! This is Responder's second bid (his rebid) and, opposite a minimum opening bid, will always indicate which "responding bracket" he is in. Coverage begins on page 39.

3 . <u>THE TWO-LEVEL</u>—This is the level of safety based on normal values typical of the average hand. Opener's *average* opening bid is minimum (13–15) and the average hand of the Responder is (6–10) which is minimum for him. When these values are present at the same time, the partnership should try to stay within the *security* of the two-level. **TWO NO-TRUMP** is considered part of the <u>three-level</u>. See diagram on page 19.

Those three definitions are the BACKBONE of Bridge, and whenever anything in this writing or in any other lesson material is referred to as BACKBONE, come back to page 21 and look again at numbers 1-2-3.

Opener Joins Responder

It's now time for the Opener and the Responder to put their hands together as best they can. This is the purpose of partnership bidding, and great satisfaction is derived from a correct and harmonious exchange of information. At all times, however, care must be taken that the partnership doesn't bid in excess of the value of the hands. Getting overboard by accident or by mis-interpretation of bids can result in harsh penalties being inflicted by the opponents. This brings us to.....THE SAFETY FACTOR of the TWO-LEVEL...which is the re-iteration of number 3, page 21. Take a look at it once again! The two-level is our level of safety. Any first bracket opening bid opposite a minimum responding hand dictates that we should not venture beyond the two-level. Respect for the safety factor is the touchstone of all constructive bidding. **BACKBONE.**

This brings us to the very important rebid by Opener. His rebid indicates the bracket in which his hand belongs . Consider this bidding sequence:

MORE BACKBONE

Opener	Responder
1♦	1♠
2♣	( )

The opening bid of 1♦ is only the hinge on which the rebid of 2♣ will swing. It says that Opener has some number of diamonds and at least 13 points including distribution. The response of 1♠ indicates at least 6 points and at least four spades. To be sure, Responder might have a much stronger hand, but that remains to be seen.

Opener rebids 2♣, which shows a club suit in addition to the diamond suit. If the description is accurate, the Responder can formulate an image of what the opening hand "looks like." NOW a critical point has been reached.

The Responder, if he prefers Opener's *first suit, is able to return to it at the two-level.* All he has to say is 2♦. However, Responder may prefer the second suit, in which case he can <u>PASS</u>.

Actually, Responder may not prefer either of Opener's suggested suits but that is immaterial at this juncture. What matters is that the Responder IS ABLE to return to Opener's first suit at the two-level if he wishes. This "courtesy," which was carefully offered by the Opener, was his way of showing a minimum-type hand. The probability of it being first bracket (13–15) is very high, although in some instances it could be second bracket (16–18).

> *This idea is formulated as a concept. Condensed into the following brief guidelines or "rules," it helps players function correctly in bidding.*

<u>**RULE FOR OPENER:**</u> Holding a *minimum* hand with two suits.... "When opening 'one of a suit,' I will plan my bidding so that after I have made my rebid, partner can go back (return) to my *original* (first-bid) suit at the two-level if he wishes. With only one suit, I will make my rebid in the same suit at the two-level or will rebid one no-trump. In no way will I *push* partner above the two-level."

<u>**RULE FOR RESPONDER:**</u> When partner makes his rebid after opening the bidding 'one of a suit,' I will ask myself, "Am I able to return to Opener's <u>FIRST</u> (or only) suit at the two-level?" If the answer is "yes," then I will know that he is showing a *minimum*-type hand.

The Opener Bids with Minimum Hands

Following are example auctions showing only the Opener's hand which illustrate the concept of Responder being able to prefer the first suit at the two-level. In each instance, Opener has shown the SIZE of his hand as well as the SHAPE.

#1.

Opener	Responder
1♦	1♥
2♣	( )

♠42
♥K3
♦AJ983
♣AQ75

#2.

Opener	Responder
1♥	1♠
2♣	( )

♠42
♥AK984
♦42
♣AJT8

#3.

Opener	Responder
1♥	1♠
1NT	( )

♠42
♥AQ865
♦KJ7
♣AT8

Hand #1 illustrates a diamond-club offering which is a true reflection of the hand. Should the Responder have a minimum, Opener wishes to play in one of these two suits. Responder CAN return to the first suit at the two-level, which suggests that the hand is minimum. The minor suit thrust indicates that both suits may be five cards long or that Opener has five diamonds and four clubs.

Hand #2 shows a heart-club offering in which the heart suit is five cards and the club suit can be either four or five. Again, Responder CAN return to Opener's first suit (hearts) at the two-level.

Hand #3 accurately displays a heart-no trump hand and again shows a minimum because Responder CAN return to the heart (only) suit at the two-level.

Fortunately, the three examples above illustrate how bidding can be constructed to accurately show partner what one holds. Now you know why the game could well be thought of as "SHOW AND TELL." It is easy to understand, but don't relax because similar examples get more difficult as you read on.

Continuing with examples which illustrate the opening bidder showing SIZE and SHAPE as defined on page 21, examine the following.

#4.

Opener	Responder
1♣	1♦
1♠	( )

♠KJ93
♥A2
♦54
♣KQ973

#5.

Opener	Responder
1♣	1♠
2♣	( )

♠A2
♥KJ93
♦54
♣KQ973

#6.

Opener	Responder
1♣	1♠
1NT	( )

♠42
♥AJ82
♦KT
♣KQ973

Hand #4 displays a club-spade hand and it must be noticed NOW that the principle of "up the ladder" is being used while the bidding is still at the one-level. The SIZE of opener's hand is either minimum or minimum-plus. He has shown his two suits in a manner which allows Responder to return to the first one at the two-level. You also know that Opener cannot have four hearts because he would have continued with the "up the ladder" concept and shown hearts before spades.

Hand #5 is of special interest because of the 2♣ rebid. This shows the SIZE to be minimum. The 1♠ response blocked out the natural heart rebid at the one-level so Opener had to make do as best he could. If he had rebid 2♥, partner would have had to bid at the three-level if he wished to return to the first suit. After a <u>one-level</u> response, if Opener forces a three-level preference, Opener should have a maximum hand, i.e., 19-plus points, including distribution.

Hand #6 is almost the same as #5, but this time the rebid is 1NT. Responder can return to the first and only suit at the two-level, which indicates Opener's SIZE, the same message as #5. The difference here is that Opener wishes to display a club-no-trump hand because he has "stoppers" in the unbid suits.

> *The reason for attaching great importance to the nuances and subtleties of inferential bidding is that, without this awareness, the partnership will often be in a gray area when making decisions. However, WITH this knowledge, one can appreciate what a partner affirmatively states or negatively implies.*

The next three examples should just about cover the various common rebids that are minimum in nature. Later, these examples will be expanded upon.

#7.

Opener	Responder
1♣	1♥
2♥	( )

♠K972
♥KQ43
♦4
♣A986

#8.

Opener	Responder
1♦	1♥
1NT	( )

♠Q97
♥42
♦AQT7
♣KQJ3

#9.

Opener	Responder
1♦	1♠
2♠	( )

♠Q97
♥4
♦AQT72
♣KQJ3

Slow down and think hard when reading the comments on these last three examples as it might seem as though there is a contradiction in concept.

Hand #7 displays a club suit-heart raise hand. Opener **DID NOT** give partner a choice of suits at the two-level. He **RAISED** Responder's suit (showing four cards). This is not the same as offering two different suits from which one should choose. Also, Opener is not obliged to call spades because the major suit fit is already found. Refer to page 14, BIDDING OBJECTIVES.

Hand #8 describes a no-trump hand after the response of 1♥. Again, this is consistent with page 14, BIDDING OBJECTIVES.

Hand #9, however, can drive some of your friends crazy when you choose the rebid of 2♠. This bid is justified despite having <u>only</u> three-card support but it isn't the ONLY correct call. In order to be consistent in the effort to execute within comfortable parameters, four-card support is expected for the immediate raise.

Consistency helps one learn to be a good player. A 2♣ rebid will drive your other friends crazy. It shows a hand that is MINIMUM and one that should play in one of your two suits (it could be correct but minors are our last choice). It is the ruffing value of the singleton heart that makes the three-card major raise look very attractive. It is also consistent with trying to play in a major. To consider a rebid of 1NT is idiocy. It implies a heart stopper which is lacking. It should be noted that a 1NT rebid **DOES NOT NECESSARILY SHOW A WEAKER HAND THAN THE REBID of 2♣ or 2♠.** It implies a different shape. Furthermore, for those souls who fear the raise of partner's response, this too is flawed. Repeating....The <u>immediate</u> raise of a known "four-card" suit promises four-card support. Again, this concept will be more fully developed later on. Nothing is perfect!

Most players should never (well, almost never) violate principles. There are four kinds of players who occasionally violate the principles set forth.

<u>**ONE**</u>: The true expert who rarely gets in trouble and who knows "when" a variation might be made. If he is wrong in the result, he takes his punishment, as does his partner, and they go on to the next hand with no recriminations or second-guessing. He bid 2♠ on hand #9. Are you in the category of the true expert?

<u>**TWO**</u>: The poor player who *thinks* he is expert because he has played for many years and he feels longevity equates to wisdom and proficiency. This is the person who ALWAYS finds a way to make his partner the "criminal."

It's almost guaranteed that you know this player because he is criticizing everything you do.

THREE: The utter fool who doesn't want to put forth any effort to get better. He is probably a decent "card-player" but at best, an average *bridge* player.

FOUR: The inexperienced player who accidentally errs when he is in the "learning process." His violations are excused, accepted and tolerated.

When competent players discuss and study bridge hands and problems, it is most remarkable how they view MOST of the game as "automatic." There should be no problem with the vast majority of bids because almost all of them fall into the category of being "automatic." This entire presentation is based on the single premise that if **YOU** understand the theoretical approach to bidding, then *almost* every hand can be bid **WITHOUT A PROBLEM!**

Opener Chooses Which Suit to Open and What He Should Rebid

The less-experienced player often finds it difficult to know with which suit to start the bidding. It is especially confusing when several people offer more than one suggestion about what is "right." It's true that occasionally a "right" bid just doesn't exist and, on other occasions, either of two choices might be "right". However, the concern you should have is for the best method to make the "right" bid most of the time. It is your obligation to show your hand to partner as best you can. This means show the SIZE and the SHAPE. You MUST accept this premise! If you cannot (or will not), it would be best if you quit right now.

Are you still here? Good! Now we can get on with it! It is a fact that in most opening-bid hands, the suit(s) will be four or five cards long. Of course, longer suits will be held once in a while, but we are talking about MOST OF THE TIME.

The most important factor when choosing the "right" suit to open is the problem of the REBID. Things seem to go rather smoothly when Opener has a five-card suit. No matter what Responder does (bidding naturally at the one-level), Opener can always rebid his suit, if necessary, or 1NT. See page 24, Hand #3 and page 25, hands #5 and #6, please. If Opener has a second suit, he will always show it, provided Responder can return to Opener's FIRST suit at the two-level.

> *You will be in the correct bidding venue when you open the bidding with a five-card major suit if you have one.*

If you have a second suit, separated from the first, it will be a minor. This is your rebid PROVIDED partner can get back to the major suit at the two-level. Look carefully at the following hands which highlight these points. Opener has separated suits! Separated suits are suits that are NOT ADJACENT to each other.

#10.

Opener	Responder
♠42	♠KQ983
♥KQJ42	♥T63
♦42	♦QJ3
♣AK63	♣72
1♥	1♠
2♣	( )

#11.

Opener	Responder
♠KQJ42	♠T82
♥2	♥A875
♦42	♦KJ98
♣AQ632	♣J7
1♠	1NT*
2♣	( )

#12.

Opener	Responder
♠42	♠KT3
♥KQJ42	♥97
♦42	♦AQ653
♣AK63	♣Q98

1♥	2♦
2♥**	

In example #10, Opener makes his natural rebid in clubs, and the Responder knows that Opener is minimum (or plus) and, because separated suits were bid, also knows Opener is 5-4 or 5-5 in his two suits. The Responder not only should "see" the Opener's nine or ten cards but should also try to "imagine" what high cards exist in that hand.

In example #11, The same situation exists for the Opener. He has shown his distribution to be nine or ten cards in the black suits with a minimum hand.

*Of special note is that Responder does NOT raise the opening spade bid with three-card support. Occasionally, the "three-card" raise can be made, but not here. The reason is that Responder has four cards in hearts and he should give Opener the opportunity to rebid the heart suit IF he has it. More on this later! Experience will assist you in seeking the four-four fit rather than the five-three fit.

In example #12, Responder has entered the two-level (to be discussed soon) and his bid BLOCKED OUT Opener's natural rebid in clubs.

**Regrettable, because Responder may think Opener has six hearts, but it must be emphasized that his hand is minimum. This is most important when drawing bidding inferences.

Which suit is bid first when Opener has ONLY four cards in his major? If the suits are separated for example, clubs-hearts, clubs-spades, or diamonds-spades, it is correct to open the minor and rebid the major PROVIDED Responder can return to the first suit at the two-level. If Responder cannot do so, then the Opener had better change his rebid. This is where things might get uncomfortable once in a while, but be aware that this problem must be faced by the greatest players as well as the average ones.

#13.

Opener	Responder
♠A2	♠K973
♥KJ93	♥T2
♦54	♦KJ982
♣KQ973	♣72
1♣	1♦
1♥	( )

#14.

Opener	Responder
♠AQ72	♠843
♥Q843	♥AJT6
♦2	♦Q743
♣AJ98	♣KT
1♣	1♦
1♥	( )

#15.

Opener	Responder
♠432	♠KQ86
♥AKJ9	♥Q65
♦J2	♦T85
♣KQ97	♣J83
1♣	1♠
INT*	

In example #13, the response of 1♦ was followed by the rebid of 1♥, which showed at least four clubs and ONLY four hearts. If the response had been 1♠, it would have **BLOCKED OUT** the heart rebid and Opener would have had to rebid 2♣. This would not permit Responder to "see" as much about the Opener's hand as desired but at least would show the SIZE—minimum.

In example #14, the response of 1♦ allowed the Opener to continue "up the ladder," and released the heart suit to Opener IF HE HAD IT, and he did. The partnership definitely benefitted in this auction and others like it because the stronger hand becomes declarer with greater frequency, which is advantageous.

In example #15, the worst scenario is produced. The only good news is that if our side plays the hand, hopefully it will be at a low-level contract.

* The spade response **BLOCKED OUT** the heart rebid and an undesirable call of 1NT is chosen by the Opener without any semblance of a diamond stopper. Yes, some opening bidders will raise to 2♠ on three small cards. Either rebid is unattractive. Making an immediate raise with three small cards is generally not attractive. So, if an alternative bid is available, use it. Making a habit of three-card raises will break down the **discipline** of a partnership.

Return to page 27 and read the text of hand #9 once again.

The effort to make the "right" call must be continual but there is no guarantee that every effort will have a successful result.

When the Opener has two suits which are adjacent to each other (touching), for example, spades-hearts, diamonds-clubs, and hearts-diamonds, a phenomenon develops for most bidders called "I JUST CAN'T DO IT"!

Learning That You Can Do It!

What is the most difficult thing for most Opening Bidders to do? The answer is: fulfilling their <u>obligation to</u>

their partners in the best way possible. This statement is not meant to be derogatory but to call attention to a very real problem which exists in bidding. The problem is that the true experts in bridge can do things "differently" or "fancy" or "systemic" as best fits their partnership. This is done by the use of different systems and/or conventions in which bids or combinations of bids might have meanings different from what is thought to be STANDARD. Even some STANDARD bidding is subject to different interpretations today. Because of the prevalence of varied interpretations, the good player understands concepts and applies them accurately to each hand.

Fulfilling an obligation to partner necessitates telling an accurate story and having partner understand what was said. Terminology and certain phrases must be understood. SIZE, SHAPE, and BIDDABLE SUIT are important to every story that is told. They are images portrayed when PROJECTING A HAND so that partner can "see it" in his mind's eye. Good bidders sometimes obtain PICTURES of the cards in partner's hand almost as if there were a large mirror behind each player and the REFLECTION could be seen from across the table.

The presentation on page 29 is an effort to lead you into this area of RESPONSIBILITY to partner. It is your absolute responsibility to bid your hand as accurately as possible so that partner can see that reflection in the imaginary mirror. When bidding suits which are separated, you were able to enjoy the merits of such careful bidding. The order of presentation of the major suit to the minor suit and vice versa allowed you to estimate the length of those suits. In addition, the order in which they were bid also allowed you to estimate his point-count. Not bad, eh?

Now let's take a more difficult proposition and try to do something similar. If you were dealt these three hands,

#16.	#17.	#18.
♠42	♠AQJ95	♠42
♥93	♥KQJ6	♥AQJ95
♦AQJ95	♦42	♦KQJ6
♣KQJ6	♣93	♣93

and were trying to describe them to any card player, wouldn't it be absolutely accurate if you described #16 as a minimum hand with two suits, diamonds and clubs? How about #17? Isn't that also a minimum hand, this time with spades and hearts? And I'm sure you would agree that #18 is also a minimum hand with two suits, in this case, hearts and diamonds.

Keeping in mind that Opener's *absolute* obligation is to bid his cards so that partner "sees" the SIZE and "sees" the SHAPE, it must be correct to open the bidding on #16 by saying 1♦ and if partner responds 1♥ or 1♠ or 1NT, Opener then rebids 2♣. Allowing Responder to return to the first suit at the two-level shows Opener's minimum size as well as his diamond-club shape to partner across the table. It's difficult to argue with that! With #17, no player can disagree with the opening bid of 1♠ and the rebid of 2♥, again showing a minimum opener and a spade-heart hand. The last hand, #18, must be opened 1♥ with the rebid of 2♦ projecting the minimum hand with hearts and diamonds.

What you just learned (hopefully) is that when holding a minimum opening hand with two biddable suits that are **TOUCHING**, it is *almost always* correct to open the HIGHER-RANKING suit and rebid the LOWER-RANKING suit. This is the ONLY way that the Opener can bid both suits in a manner that properly projects SIZE and SHAPE to Responder. *"Almost always" assumes the suits are BIDDABLE.*

Now let's study the same three hands with a single card being taken from one of the biddable suits and put into the other.

#19.	#20.	#21.
♠42	♠AQJ9	♠42
♥93	♥KQJ65	♥AQJ9
♦AQJ9	♦42	♦KQJ65
♣KQJ65	♣93	♣93

The five-spot has been removed from the original five-card suit and placed in the lower-ranking suit to make it the five-carder. However, if you look at the hands and try to describe them to the same partner or to any other card-player, how would you do it? Let me answer the question for you! You would describe hand #19 exactly as you did hand #16. You would describe hand #20 exactly as you did hand #17. And, dear reader, you would describe hand #21 the same as hand #18. The three hands are still two-suiters.

Therefore, as a concept, it MUST be concluded that it is correct to bid the hands in the same way by opening the HIGHER-RANKING suit and rebidding the LOWER-RANKING suit. The only proviso is the need that the HIGHER RANKING suit, if it is only four cards long, must be a very good biddable suit!!!

This doesn't alter the system (called "Five-card Majors) that, when a major suit is opened, it will be five cards long. In fact, without playing that system, whenever a major suit is opened, percentage-wise, it will be five cards. In actual play, using the concept solves one of the awkward bidding problems that exist. Remember, all hands can't be bid to perfection, but all hands CAN be bid to show SIZE correctly and to show SHAPE with reasonable accuracy. The safety of the TWO-LEVEL and consideration for Responder influences the entire concept. Therefore, it is correct to assume that whenever a major suit is opened, it will be five cards long. The EXCEPTION is when the higher of touching suits contains four GOOD cards and Opener must plan his rebid ahead of time. YOU CAN DO IT!

The selection of the initial thrust MUST be grounded on the probable course of FUTURE BIDDING. By starting with 1♠ on hand #20, the heart suit may be safely introduced on the rebid without advancing the auction beyond the two-level. It is totally illogical to argue that a player can introduce a four-card suit at the two or three-level and not be allowed to introduce the same suit at the one-level.

CHAPTER FOUR

THE RESPONDING HAND

L ike his partner, Responder considers two matters: He must decide whether he has the values to reply and, if so, he must select a form for his description. In choosing, Responder is influenced by the identical concepts (**BACK-BONE)** that guide the Opener.

Very little has been developed concerning the Responder and the concepts which guide him through the bidding process. On pages 19 and 20, the idea of "up the ladder" bidding was submitted. When responding, one should bid within a predetermined framework. This idea is called "THE CONCEPT OF PREDETERMINATION," and is explained as follows. While a player is sorting and arranging his cards, he should count the number of high-card and distributional points in the hand. Imagine that you were dealt ♠Q9763 ♥Q74 ♦K53 ♣32. When sorting the hand and arranging the suits, you counted seven points in high cards and eight points when including distribution. According to the **SAFETY FACTOR** and the fact that most opening bids are of minimum value, if partner opens and shows a minimum, you are entitled to bid only one time with these cards. This is your PREDETERMINED "right" and **OBLIGATION.**

The Responder must think of his responsibilities and obligations before the bidding starts. After the cards are dealt, count your values and say to yourself...**IF MY PARTNER OPENS THE BIDDING AND SHOWS A TRUE-MINIMUM HAND, I WILL BID AS MANY TIMES AS MY POINT-COUNT TELLS ME I MUST.**

With:	Responder will make:
[six to ten points]	One bid
[eleven or twelve points]	Two Bids
[thirteen or more points]	Get us to GAME!

The words "call" and "bid" must be differentiated. Responder may call (speak) two or even three times and make only one bid. He may be forced to "bid" again. This may seem confusing but is explained on page eleven. If he takes a simple preference for one of partner's suits, he is NOT showing additional SIZE, just a part of his SHAPE.

The PREDETERMINED number of bids by Responder is predicated on Opener showing a minimum hand. If Opener shows extra values, bidding changes occur.

A BID by Responder shows SIZE (point count) and, to some degree, SHAPE. However, his SHAPE is rather vague in the beginning of an auction. A difficult area of Bridge is listening to a Responder speak and "de-coding" his words to know whether he BID showing values or whether he BID just making a "call."

When Responder has bid, he may have shown a hand with "limited" point-count or one with "unlimited" count. A LIMITED BID for either partner is one in which the lowest and highest point-count of the hand is known! For instance, an opening 1NT bid (which we have not mentioned before) is limited because the stated lowest value is 16 H.C.points and the highest value is 18 H.C. points.

There are three calls which the Responder can make which are, or might be, categorized as ONE-bid (limited) hands. Opener's hand is unseen.

#22.

Opener	Responder
	♠K96
????	♥42
	♦K9742
	♣Q65
1♥	1NT

#23.

Opener	Responder
	♠42
????	♥KJ85
	♦842
	♣K873
1♣	1♥

#24.

Opener	Responder
	♠42
????	♥432
	♦K874
	♣AJ63
1♦	2♦

In hand #22, the Responder's 1NT call is a BID showing 6-10 points (a limited bid) in high cards for SIZE and denies four hearts or four spades for SHAPE. If you train yourself to think of the inferences, this bid also indicates either a diamond or a club suit, or both.

In hand #23, Responder's 1♥ bid shows four cards in hearts and at least six points. This "new suit" by Responder at the one-level is unlimited in point count. Responder may have greater values and is planning to make more than just this BID. If he has greater strength, his subsequent actions may be determined by what the Opener says with his rebid.

In hand #24, Responder's call of 2♦ shows a limited count of 6-10 points <u>including</u> distribution. The SIZE is known and the SHAPE is partly known by inference. Responder should not have either four spades or four hearts.

Responder Bids Again

It is sometimes difficult to "know" when Responder has BID a second or a third time. He may speak (call) more than once but BID only one time. The more times that he BIDS, the more count he promises. Study auctions #25, #26, and #27. YOU determine how many bids Responder made and how many points he has!

#25.

Opener	Responder
1♣	1♥
1♠	2♣

#26.

Opener	Responder
1♣	1♥
1♠	1NT

#27.

Opener	Responder
1♣	1♥
1♠	2♥

In the above auctions, Responder spoke (bid) twice in each example, but BID (showing values) only once. Did you think otherwise?

In the first instance, he showed a preference for partner's first suit (clubs) and a desire to quit within the safety of the two-level. More **BACKBONE.**

In the second example, he showed an inclination for no-trump play and again made no effort to venture out of the safety the two-level.

In the last auction, Responder rejected a selection of one of Opener's suits and instead chose his own. The inference is that hearts is the best place to play despite the fact that Opener made no promise of help in that suit. Notice that the partnership is still within the safety of the two-level.

So, how do we recognize when RESPONDER BIDS AGAIN? By definition:

When the Responder bids a "new suit" at the one-level and Opener rebids showing a minimum-type hand, if Responder (making his rebid) introduces another "new suit" (forcing) OR takes the partnership past the **TWO-LEVEL, HE HAS MADE ANOTHER BID!**

If Responder's second bid is in a "new suit," it is FORC-ING (with one exception explained in the next paragraph) and it shows at least 11 points. If the Responder's second bid is not in a "new suit", it is NON-FORCING and he has precisely 11 or 12 points. When he bids a suit, distribution is counted, but if his second bid is two no-trump, it shows 11 or 12 high-card points. Whenever the Responder makes a second bid which is non-forcing, it is called an "Invitational" or "Chance-Giving" Bid.

The exception to the "new suit" by Responder being a FORCE is, **that, if the auction is interrupted by the call of 1NT, either as a rebid by Opener OR a bid by the opponent, the FORCE is off**. However, a "reverse" in the order of bidding or a "jump" in a new suit is still forcing.

Within this framework, an Invitational bid says, "I don't have enough strength to get you to game if you have the barest minimum opening bid of thirteen points. However, if you have a QUEEN more than you promised, accept the Invitation and bid game." In other words, the Responder gives the Opener one more "chance," hence "Chance-Giving."

Here are six examples of Responder's hands opposite a phantom opening bid. The auction is shown and each underlined bid has to be known. It is vital to the understanding of Bridge. The key bids are marked with one or more asterisks and are explained following the hands. You should determine which bids are *limited, unlimited, forcing, non-forcing,* or *invitational.*

#28.

Opener	Responder
	♠42
????	♥AQT982
	♦K6
	♣Q43
1♦	1♥
1NT	3♥*

#29.

Opener	Responder
	♠KJ742
????	♥AQT93
	♦4
	♣Q2
1♦	1♠
2♣	2♥**

#30.

Opener	Responder
	♠Q9743
????	♥2
	♦KJ852
	♣42
1♥	1♠
1NT	2♦***

#31.

Opener	Responder
	♠KJ743
????	♥42
	♦42
	♣AQ85
1♦	1♠
2♣	3♣*

#32.

Opener	Responder
	♠K952
????	♥Q85
	♦AQ85
	♣42
1♥	1♠
2♥	3♥*

#33.

Opener	Responder
	♠42
	♥KQ85
????	♦AQ9
	♣JT32

1♣	1♥
1♠	2NT*

*   Invitational or Chance-Giving...11 or 12...Nonforcing
** New Suit...Forcing...At least 11...Unlimited
*** New Suit...But nonforcing...Auction interrupted by 1NT...LIMITED 6–10.

The preceding six hands illustrate much of what one should understand regarding the obligations and actions of the Responder opposite minimum rebids by the Opener. Responding actions are predetermined, and all good players understand the concept. At this point, a solid foundation has been set forth for you. Learning and recognizing the concepts takes some time and effort. Moreover, it requires some "thinking." Let these ideas become automatic and you will find yourself in a most enjoyable entertainment avenue.

Bridge is easily the finest leisure pursuit. It presents a stimulating challenge, an opportunity to meet people from different walks of life, a means for having "something to do," an opportunity to enter into "competition" which some people just love, and above all, it keeps the "gray matter" working so it doesn't waste away.

CHAPTER FIVE

THE OPENER REBIDS WITH MAXIMUM HANDS

On page 23 rules for both Opener and Responder were carefully presented. Care was taken to ease the learning process for you and, at the same time, to make you aware of the need for caution in bidding. Great emphasis was placed on the safety of the TWO-LEVEL. On page 38 and thereafter, we discussed Responder's actions and emphasized his making only one bid with six-ten points.

Tight reins were put on the partnership because neither hand might have had the strength to venture into the DANGER ZONE which is the three-level. When bidding any two-suited hand, Opener will use the three-level to show a MAXIMUM hand. The count which is needed by Opener for this action is 19 points, including distribution.

The messages sent by the example auctions on pages 24-27 were similar in that they all showed minimums. Changing or adding high cards often alters the auction as far as Opener is concerned. Some of the following examples are similar in distribution to those on pages 24-27, so you might find it useful to compare them to each other.

#34.

Opener	Responder
1♦	1♥
3♣	( )

♠42
♥K3
♦AKQ93
♣AK75

#35.

Opener	Responder
1♥	1♠
3♣	( )

♠42
♥AKQ98
♦42
♣AKQJ

#36.

Opener	Responder
1♥	1♠
2NT	( )

♠AJ
♥AQ865
♦KJ7
♣AT8

Hand #34 displays a diamond-club offering which shows the SHAPE of the hand. More important, however, is that the Responder **CANNOT** return to Opener's **first** suit at the TWO-LEVEL. That fact, and only that, is the method by which Opener shows that the SIZE of his hand is **MAXIMUM**. The safety of the two-level was violated when the second suit was introduced and the player who caused this is obliged to have a terrific hand which warrants entry into the danger zone. The partnership is now committed to continue bidding until game is reached. That auction by Opener is called a JUMP SHIFT and, opposite the response (at least six points), the partnership has at least 26 points. A Jump Shift, after any response, creates a **GAME FORCE**.

Hand #35 shows another Jump Shift auction with Opener having at least five hearts and four clubs. Again, the partnership is in a Game Force. The poor Responder might have only a meager hand but he must continue bidding because of the "force."

Hand #36 introduces a heart-no-trump hand of great strength because Responder cannot return to Opener's (only) suit at the two-level. This bid is called a JUMP TAKE-OUT as opposed to a JUMP SHIFT. The latter is comprised of a Jump and a Shift to another suit while the former is a Jump and a Take-out from a suit to no-trump. The Jump Take-out reflects only High Card points. It is conceivable that the response of 1♠ was made with an Ace and two doubletons, which gave that bidder six points. In reality, he has only four HIGH CARD points for no-trump play. If he decides that the hand should play in no-trump, he can pass.

When bidding suits, the distributional points are counted, but when bidding NO-TRUMP, only high cards are counted. Therefore, a jump-shift does not always promise 19 points in high cards. Three more examples further illustrate the rebid action of the Opener.

#37.

Opener	Responder
1♣	1♦
2♠	( )

♠AQ93
♥A2
♦54
♣AKQ97

#38.

Opener	Responder
1♣	1♠
2♥	( )

♠A2
♥AKQ9
♦54
♣KQ976

#39.

Opener	Responder
1♣	1♥
2♦	( )

♠A2
♥42
♦AKQ7
♣KQ976

Hand #37 is a classic in which Opener shows a MAXI-MUM hand because (I hope you guessed it) Responder **cannot** return to Opener's first bid suit at the two-level. Opener bid SIZE! At this point, the bidding sequence shows the SHAPE of four or five clubs and four spades.

Hand #38 is most interesting because the 1♠ response blocked out the natural heart rebid at the one-level. With a minimum hand such as the example (#5) on page 25, Opener had to rebid his club suit. However, with this extra strength, he can rebid the heart suit to show SIZE. Partner **cannot** return to the first suit at the two-level. As in the previous example, the bidding reflects Opener's SHAPE to be four or five clubs and four hearts at this point.

With hand #39, the same phenomenon occurs regarding the choice of suits at the TWO-LEVEL. Can Responder return to Opener's first suit at the TWO-LEVEL? NO! That shows Opener's SIZE to be maximum and the SHAPE is guaranteed to be **LONGER** clubs than diamonds. The bidding sequence which took place is called a "REVERSE" because in natural bidding, if the suits are touching and the hand is minimum, it is usually better to bid the higher-ranking suit before the lower-ranking suit. Here the natural procedure was reversed, hence the name.

Starting on page 29, five-and-a-half pages were devoted to choosing the correct suit with which to open the bidding. The entire concept was conceived to handle the average SIZE hand and to utilize the safety of the TWO-LEVEL when necessary.

Important

RULE FOR OPENER: With Maximum hands, open the longer suit and rebid the shorter one. If the suits are equal in length, open the same one you would have opened if the hand were minimum. However, change your rebid so Responder **cannot** return to the first bid suit at the two-level.

In each of the following examples, Responder has a "one-bid" hand opposite any minimum opening bid, BUT...

#40.

Opener	Responder
♠42	♠KQ983
♥AKQJ4	♥T63
♦42	♦QJ3
♣AKJ3	♣72

1♥	1♠
3♣	3♥
4♥	

#41.

Opener	Responder
♠KQJ42	♠982
♥KQJ2	♥A875
♦42	♦KJ9
♣AQ	♣953

1♠	1NT?
3♥	4♥

#42.

Opener	Responder
♠KQJ42	♠T8
♥KQJ2	♥875
♦42	♦AQ93
♣AQ	♣JT43

1♠	1NT
3♥	3NT

In hand #40, the Responder makes his initial call of 1♠. After hearing the Jump Shift which puts on the "game force," he shows his heart preference and Opener (having shown his hand) bids the game and trusts he can play it and lose no more than three tricks. Responder, with his poor hand never dreamed of game.

Hand #41 is a simple 1NT response, but some players would wrongly raise to 2♠. With flat distribution, a raise on three cards seems less attractive. Other players <u>always</u> raise to 2♠, and admittedly, this poses a "?" regarding the correct action since Opener might have a hand of spades and hearts. Sure enough, the heart rebid comes as a Jump Shift and the happy raise to 4♥ follows. Check page 30, example #11. Look at Responder's hand and review the explanation.

Hand #42 shows another 1NT bid. After Opener's Jump Shift, Responder is honor bound not to pass. He might be correct to take a preference to spades with his doubleton. He might consider an immediate raise in hearts without four. Voila! He calls 3NT, although 3♠ is acceptable. If the doubleton contains an honor, the preference to the opening suit becomes a superior choice.

CHAPTER SIX

THE OPENER REBIDS WITH A MINIMUM-PLUS (16–18) HAND

When Opener holds a second bracket hand of 16-18 points, there are some bids which immediately and accurately describe both his SIZE and SHAPE. One of the most commonly used is an opening bid of 1NT which shows a balanced hand with at least three suits "stopped." A STOPPER is any card or combination of cards that prohibits the opponents from taking all the tricks in a given suit. Another specific example regarding Opener's SIZE and SHAPE is the Jump Rebid in his own suit. A third example which shows Opener's SIZE and SHAPE is an immediate Jump Raise of Responder's suit. Three hands that follow illustrate the above.

#43.

Opener	Responder
♠KJ	♠T854
♥AT73	♥K2
♦KQ8	♦9765
♣AT85	♣K97

1NT	Pass

#44.

Opener	Responder
♠42	♠AJ953
♥AJ9	♥432
♦AKJT85	♦2
♣K6	♣QT75

1♦	1♠
3♦	Pass

#45.

Opener	Responder
♠KJ85	♠T9432
♥AQ	♥J43
♦AJT43	♦82
♣42	♣AJ8

1♦	1♠
3♠	Pass

Hand #43 is a classic 1NT opening bid and Responder has a normal Pass. With less strength, the Pass would still be in order, perhaps with a little prayer.

Hand #44 is another classic. Opener's Jump Rebid shows a good six or seven-card suit with 16-18 points including distribution. **The Jump Rebid by Opener may be made with 6½ or 7 "playing tricks" with the bid suit as trumps!** Many players feel that an opening hand (with a good long suit) which counts to 6½ playing tricks is the "equivalent" of second bracket. Playing tricks will be discussed in detail later on.

Hand #45 is a Jump Raise in Responder's suit. Opener would have raised the response to 2♠ with a minimum hand (13-15) and would have raised to game with a maximum (19-21).

In each of the three examples, the SIZE of Opener's hand is identical. However, the SHAPE of each is different.

The first hand is bid to indicate a balanced SHAPE. The

second hand, after the rebid, indicates the SHAPE of a long-suiter. The third hand, again after the rebid, indicates the SHAPE of four-card spade support with four or more diamonds.

Showing a second bracket by using any of the above auctions is easy to learn.

Additionally, some second bracket opening hands must be bid as if they are True Minimums but, given an opportunity, **ONE MORE BID WILL BE MADE**. It is the "one more" bid, voluntarily made, which says, "I have a little extra." Consider the following examples in which Opener first shows a minimum hand, then, when given the opportunity, makes "one more bid" to indicate the extra values.

#46

Opener	Responder
♠2	♠AT975
♥KQJ42	♥953
♦K42	♦AQ
♣AQ85	♣J2

1♥	1♠
2♣	2♥
3♥*	?

#47.

Opener	Responder
♠T8	♠KJ9743
♥AQJ43	♥52
♦AQ	♦K63
♣KT85	♣J7

1♥	1♠
2♣	2♠
2NT*	?

#48.

Opener	Responder
♠Q53	♠KJT942
♥AQJ43	♥2
♦4	♦K63
♣AK85	♣Q92

1♥	1♠
2♣	2♠
3♠*	?

* In each instance, the asterisk denotes the bid which says "I have extra values." In Hand #46, after Responder's heart preference, Opener made "one more bid" to show the added values of a MINIMUM-PLUS hand. This "invitational" or "chance-giving" bid shows second bracket and urges partner to bid game IF he has the upper portion of his stated values.

In Hand #47, the bid of 2NT is the "added value" call and, because it is in NT, all the values are high-card points. It shows good stoppers in the unbid suit, diamonds. The NT call also promises a doubleton spade and is "invitational." Only experts make voluntary bids in NT with singletons. Avoid this if you can.

In Hand #48, The 3♠ bid verifies a singleton or void in diamonds in addition to the extra values. Didn't Opener show five hearts, at least four clubs, and now three spades? The "chance-giving" bid can be passed but, with his hand, Responder should bid game.

In each example, Opener has revealed the exact SIZE and almost the exact SHAPE of his hand. Note that with the exception of Hand #43, each auction and the representative hands demonstrate a delayed bid which takes the partnership through the comfort and safety of the TWO-LEVEL.

This "violation" should create an impact on you in respect to the BACKBONE of Bridge. Proper understanding of each bid, and learning to "see" an accurate reflection of a bidding hand, makes the game fun.

Remember, YOU must be responsible for accurately projecting your cards to your PARTNER.
Always bid for partner, never for yourself!!!!!!!!
SHOW AND TELL.

CHAPTER SEVEN

RESPONDER ENTERS THE TWO-LEVEL

When Responder bids a new suit at the one-level, more often than not he will have a "one-bid" hand. Of course, he may have more count but, at the moment, it cannot be presumed. If Responder bids 1NT, he has 6-10 high-card points.

There are times when he will enter the TWO-LEVEL with his bid. If his bid is a "raise" of partner's suit, Responder usually promises four* or more cards in the suit and 6-10 points including distribution. There is a distinction between "entering" the two-level which is in a new suit and "raising" partner's suit to the two-level.

Of utmost importance is when Responder enters the two-level in a **NEW SUIT**. Entering the TWO-LEVEL tells a big story. In this game of "SHOW AND TELL," an error in this area of bidding can prove to be disastrous. Remember, you are bidding for partner's benefit and he will be decoding (hopefully) each message that you send. The rules of bridge don't allow you to gasp or say "I'm

---

*It is a generally accepted principle that four-card support is usually necessary when making an IMMEDIATE raise. There are exceptions, of course, but not many, and this principle does not apply to defensive bidding.

sorry" while an auction is going on. So if you erred in sending a message and partner gets in deep trouble because of it, please:

GO DIRECTLY TO JAIL! DO NOT PASS GO! DO NOT DO ANYTHING BUT GO DIRECTLY TO PAGE 1 AND START AGAIN! BUT, ABOVE ALL, PLEASE DO NOT TELL <u>ANYONE</u> THAT YOU LEARNED FROM ME!!

Conceptually, when Responder enters the two-level in a new suit, he shows at least 11 points, no fewer than 10 of which are in HIGH CARDS. Exceptions in count are sometimes made, but as a general rule, this concept is always in effect. When Responder enters the two-level in a new suit, he indicates possession of a hand which is worth at least two bids and it PROMISES that he will bid again. By unspoken agreement, the bidding indicates that the hand is "ours" and that we might bid a game.

The late Lawrence Weiss of Boston, in his classic book *Bidding Structure*, eloquently expressed this concept as follows: "By bidding at the two-level, the Responder not only guarantees sufficient capital for that venture, but signs at the same time a promissory note for an additional undertaking." Right on target!

New and intermediate players are amazed when good players draw accurate conclusions about unseen hands. It is no trick. A good player listens to each bid, puts them in his "mental de-coder" and develops a picture which is rather clear. When you understand concepts such as the conditions for Responder "entering the two-level," it can almost guarantee your success in being a competent bridge player. The two example hands which follow are similar but must be bid differently. In both instances the opening bid is 1♥. The Responder holds:

#49.			#50.	
	♠42			♠Q42
????	♥KJ3		????	♥3
	♦42			♦QT
	♣AQT742			♣AJT7432

Opener	Responder		Opener	Responder
1♥	2♣		1♥	1NT
2♥	3♥		2♥	3♣

It is not necessary to show the Opener's cards which are irrelevant. In #49, if you are the Opener and "heard" partner's bid of 2♣, you are alerted to his entering the two-level and that he has the values to do so. You know that he (1) has at least 10 high-card points, (2) he will make another bid, and (3) he has five clubs. In some instances, he may have only four clubs, but this is immaterial as he will bid again. See page 38, and note the CONCEPT OF PREDETERMINATION, which is thoroughly discussed on the next page. After the rebid of 2♥, his raise to 3♥ shows 11 or 12 points. It is a classic hand with which Responder bid twice. His invitational bid suggests that partner re-examine his hand. If Responder had the values of an opening bid, instead of calling 3♥ he would have called 4♥.

In the second example, Responder's bid of 1NT limits the hand to 10 points in high cards. After Opener's rebid, the 3♣ bid indicates the desire to make IT the final contract. It is illogical and unreasonable to think that Responder would raise the level of bidding and go from a major suit to a minor suit if (1) he had help in hearts or (2) he had only five clubs. This auction shows both a very long club suit and a deficiency in partner's suit.

Two paragraphs above, it is stated that Responder has five cards in clubs when he enters the two-level, but a bit further on, it says that he may have only four. This is a very important matter that should be discussed NOW.

In natural bidding, an opening bid might cause Responder to enter the two-level if he wishes to bid a new suit which is **lower** in rank than Opener's suit. Opposite many opening bids in a suit, there is room at the one-level for Responder to bid when his suit is **higher** ranking, even if it is only four cards long. When responding to a 1♠ opener, it is an unwritten "law" that if the response is 2♥, it promises five cards, but if the response is 2♣ or 2♦, it promises (?) because the Responder might have a difficult bidding problem. Too few players handle this situation correctly. Of the many links in the chain that make bridge, the one called THE CONCEPT OF PREDETERMINATION solves most bidding problems.

Do you recall which bid is the second most important bid in Bridge? This is another **BACKBONE** situation, which are what pages 22–24 is all about. If you have preconceived ideas about bidding and/or the use of special conventions, please put them aside and allow a concept to evolve which should make bidding much easier. This is where we fully develop.

The Concept of Predetermination

All bidding methods are designed to bid whatever cards that are dealt to the best contract. On each hand, a partnership "hopes" to have the combined strength to reach game. Reaching game, or falling short, should reflect the SIZE of the combined hands. The partnership minds must work as one in this endeavor. Regarding a final contract, it is **PREDETERMINED** that the order of preference is to play in a MAJOR SUIT, NO-TRUMP, or a MINOR SUIT, in that order. The final contract depends on the SHAPE of the combined hands. For the final contract to be a MAJOR SUIT GAME, proper conditions must exist. Two example hands are given: the first is for an Opening Bidder and the second is for a Responder. Be careful! The hands are separate entities and do NOT belong as partners.

<u>#51.</u>

As an Opener, <u>you</u> have:
- ♠J72
- ♥KQJ85
- ♦2
- ♣AK73

<u>#52.</u>

As a Responder, <u>you</u> have:
- ♠J974
- ♥K6
- ♦AT842
- ♣K5

With #51, you, the OPENER, should think about and PREDETERMINE the conditions of the final contract before the bidding starts. Talk to yourself. Create a silent monologue which would go something like this:

Well, here I am with a very nice opening bid. If partner has a hand worth "two bids" (11 or 12 points), we will bid to game in hearts IF he has three-card support. If we fail to agree on hearts, we will reach a spade game IF he has five of them. If neither major contract exists, we will settle for no-trump provided he has diamond and spade cards. If nothing good happens, we may be in trouble.

The importance of this is that the partnership is seeking a major suit-fit and knows the conditions with which it can be reached. That is, (1) four opposite four, (2) five opposite three, and (3) six opposite two. It is a PREDETERMINED target.

The no-trump target is also PREDETERMINED provided the major suit-fit doesn't exist and if the partnership has stoppers in all four suits. A minor suit-fit might exist, but that is frequently by-passed to play in no-trump because fewer tricks are needed to make a game.

With #52, you, the Responder, start your own monologue. Do yourself a favor. Say it to yourself and don't move your lips or else people will think my teaching is driving you crazy. It might go something like this:

> *Here I am with a pretty good hand. I certainly hope my partner opens the bidding. If he does, and bids minimum, I will bid TWICE because I have 11 or 12 points and am committed to make two bids opposite any minimum opener. We will play in (1) spades if he has four, (2) hearts if he has six, or (3) no-trump and hope for the best. If he bids minimum, my second bid will be Invitational; that is, one short of game. I hope he remembers to bid the game if he has a Queen more than he promised.*

In summation, the CONCEPT OF PREDETERMINATION always encourages each half of the partnership to consider a "place to play" (target) and "how high to bid" before an auction actually begins.

The second most important bid is Responder's Rebid. The following examples are Responder's hands only and illustrate his rebid action, how it is thought out, and why a bid is chosen.

#53.

Opener	Responder
	♠Q85
????	♥KQ97
	♦9853
	♣A8
1♣	1♦
?	?

#54.

Opener	Responder
	♠A6
????	♥K85
	♦KJ63
	♣9873
1♠	2♣
?	2NT

#55.

Opener	Responder
	♠KJ53
????	♥J73
	♦AK5
	♣862
1♠	2♣*
?	3♠

With Hand #53, the response of 1♦ begins the "up-the-ladder" process of bidding and releases the heart and spade rebids to Opener. If Opener rebids 1♥, Responder's rebid is 3♥, Chance-Giving. If Opener rebids either 1♠ or 1NT or 2♣, Responder's second bid is 2NT, also Chance-Giving. The entire sequence is **PREDETERMINED**.

With Hand #54, after the opening 1♠ bid, Responder bids 2♣ which is the "cheapest" bid available. This might provoke a gasp and questions about someone's state of mind, but follow the thinking through to see if it makes sense. The fact that Responder entered the two-level is an *impact* bid indicating at least 11 points and the promise to bid again. Also, the bid allows Opener the freedom of the two-level in which to make any minimum rebid. Regardless of what it is, Responder intends to bid 2NT as his second, and Chance-Giving, bid. 2NT was predetermined to be the second call, which is the key to the example. The first bid was relatively unimportant but it enabled the second call to be made. Responder might have done the partnership a great service in the eventual play of the hand. Why is this so? Because the defense will probably avoid a club lead!

This bid is not intended as a "crazy" or "psychic" bid. "Crazy" bids are for crazy people and "psychic" bids are for psychotics who do great harm to the game. This can be classified as a "temporizing" bid, which is more clearly illustrated in the next explanation.

*With Hand #55, when partner opened 1♠, Responder <u>knew</u> his second bid might be 3♠ which is Invitational or Chance-Giving. He had to make **some** bid before he could make his second one. He couldn't bid 2♥ which promised five cards, so, out of necessity, he bid a three-card suit. By entering the two-level in either clubs or diamonds, he showed that he is going to bid again. Opener will think that Responder has a "real" suit, but it <u>CANNOT</u> affect Opener in any way. After Opener's rebid, whatever it is, Responder bids spades, setting the contract in that suit. Since Responder had to enter the level of two in his initial response, he had to "temporize." If he is going to temporize, then he should try to channel the defense for partner's benefit.

Perhaps the idea of "temporizing" has never been explained to you. Most players, including those new to the game, have been exposed to it in another form. Regardless of the bidding method used, Opener's rebid is of prime importance. The opening bidder will frequently begin the auction with a "three-card" club suit, often referred to as a "short" or "convenient" club. In all probability, you and your friends have done it thousands of times. What you did was "temporize" or "build a bid into your hand," which allowed an easier rebid. This is commonplace, not fancy and not unique. However, this is probably the first time you have ever had it explained or taught to you in concept or as theory.

These pages should make you aware that any two players can create and build a partnership of reasonable competence. The theory of the game and the concepts which apply must be understood. We have examined Opener's and Responder's obligations and have seen that the prospects for arriving at sound contracts are substantially enhanced by disciplined choices, by predetermined concepts, and by the somewhat elusive presumption of fit. The introduction of more powerful responses will bring this portion of bidding to a close.

The opponents have been left out of the bidding so the proper framework between Opener and Responder could be presented without interference.

Responder Has Opening-Bid Values!

There are times when partner opens the bidding and you (the Responder) also have the values of an opening bid. The "up-the-ladder" concept still applies for one-level responses, but IF you respond in a new suit at the one-level and partner rebids minimum, you must either "force" by bidding another new suit or go directly to game. You must plan your bids very carefully in order to display your "three-bid" (13–15 points) hand. **PREDETERMINATION!** However, there are some "three-bid" hands which can be shown with one bid.

One of these is the Jump Raise in partner's suit. This bid shows 13–16 points including distribution, which means the actual high-card points could be as few as 12 but no more than 15. Another strength-showing bid is the Jump Take-out to 2NT. This bid shows 13–15 high-card points and follows the "up-the-ladder" concept fully. The following examples illustrate these bids WITH variations, yet no concepts are violated. The Jump Raise always shows at least four-card support for partner, and the Jump Take-out always shows stoppers in the other suits.

These are your hands as RESPONDER:

#56.	#57.	#58.	#59.
♠A6	♠A975	♠42	♠AJ4
♥KJ97	♥K2	♥A97	♥KQ8
♦AT853	♦AQ83	♦AQ83	♦9742
♣42	♣964	♣K964	♣K96

#56. This is your hand in response to partner's 1♥ Opener. The only bid is 3♥. The Jump Raise shows both your values and four-card support. If partner had opened 1♣, you would have bid 1♦, and if he had opened 1♦, you would have bid 1♥. Both sequences are consistent with the "up-the-ladder" or "one-over-one" concept. Of course, if he had opened with 1♠, you would have bid 2♦.

#57. This is your hand in response to partner's opening bid of 1♦. Your first bid is (only) 1♠ despite your full opening-bid values. The concept of "one-over-one" should be adhered to so that the major suit-fit can be easily found if it exists. Conceptually, bidding 3♦ is absurd as it violates procedure and also "lies" about the SHAPE.

#58. With this hand in response to a 1♦ opening, the best bid is 3♦ showing the correct values with the diamond fit. It also denies a major suit AND the ability to call NT. Something isn't "stopped."

#59. In response to a 1♦ opening, this is a classic 2NT bid. It shows the high-card count AND the stoppers in all suits.

With hands #56, #58, and #59, the Responder's call is limited and establishes the Opener as CAPTAIN of the hand.

Responder's Jump Shift

The Jump Shift by Responder is a special bid which is often misused. There are two conditions which should be met in order to Jump Shift. The #1 requirement is the SIZE of the hand. It should be no fewer than 17 points in high cards. With distribution, it should count to no less than 19. The #2 requirement is SHAPE. However, unlike other SHAPE, this is a promise that you have a "place to play" the hand. A "place to play" means either a self-sufficient suit of your own with which you made the Jump Shift or a terrific "fit" in partner's suit. When a Jump Shift is made, the partnership should consider bidding slam. Some players agree that a "try" for slam must be made after any Jump Shift and the "place to play" is known.

You can probably recall many instances in your life when you excitedly tried to get someone's attention. Perhaps you called loudly and were not heard or you waved wildly and were not seen. Getting someone's attention is what the Jump Shift is all about. The bid itself comes in two parts. The first part is the jump in response to the opening bid and that call is the "attention getter." The second call is the "place to play." It is possible to have many hands start out with the same "attention getter" and end up in different places. For instance...

#60.	#61.	#62.
♠AK2	♠Q75	♠AQJ
♥KQ972	♥3	♥43
♦42	♦AK8	♦AKQ2
♣AQ5	♣AKQJ84	♣K432

You are the Responder with these hands. In each instance partner opened with 1♥. With #60, you could bid either 2♠, 3♣, or 3♦ (temporizing). It doesn't matter which suit you chose. Your desire was to get partner's attention. After he rebids, you will bid hearts to establish the "place to play" and the bidding goes on.

In the next example, #61, you Jump Shift in clubs, and after partner's rebid, you repeat clubs setting the "place to play." Certainly the suit is self-sufficient.

In hand #62, you again Jump Shift in clubs and after partner's rebid (presumably 3♥), the bid of 3NT shows the "place to play." It is not expected that partner will pass. Although the no-trump call describes the "place to play," Opener will continue bidding toward a slam either in no-trump or in his suit. If you wonder why the choice of jumps was the club suit rather than the diamond suit, turn to hands #54 and #55 starting on page 60.

Thoughts Concerning Five-Card Majors

All players open "five-card majors," but it is an incorrect assumption that one can NEVER open with only "four cards" in the major suit. In natural bidding, when an opening bid is made in a major suit, it will usually be five cards long. This is true a very high percentage of the time. However, Responder should always *presume* that the suit is five cards long. If an opening major suit bid guarantees that the suit is five cards long, this is most effective when used as part of a systemic method of bidding called "Five-Card Majors with a One No-trump Response Forcing." The use of this method enjoins the partnership to alter the basic bidding structure.

There are reasons to support and defend the use of "FIVE-CARD MAJORS."

When playing the method called FIVE-CARD MAJORS, it gives added confidence to those players who have a reluctance or fear about playing a hand when holding *only* a four-card trump suit. It also allows Responder's bidding problems to become somewhat simplified when there is competitive bidding. Of course, the simplification exists primarily when he has major suit assistance. He can raise immediately with only three-card support. Without ample support, intricate artificial bids must be learned and employed to assist in getting to a correct contract.

In actual practice, a very high percentage of top players who use this method eagerly open a "four-card" major in third and fourth position. They will often do so in first or second position when it is necessary to prepare a re-bid.

There are several logical arguments *against* the use of "FIVE-CARD MAJORS."

First, it forces the opening bidder to make frequent prepared and slightly unnatural bids in the minor suits. This is especially true when the Opener has a club shortage with two four-card major suits.

Second, whenever an opening bid is made in a minor suit, the Responder often has to guess what to do when he has support for that minor because he has doubts whether the opening suit is "real." He may be reluctant to assist without at least five cards in the minor suit.

Third, when the opening bid is 1♦ and the response is 2♣, Opener's natural rebid is often "blocked out". His rebid becomes difficult and the concepts concerning a "reverse" bid and a preference at the two-level must be altered.

Fourth, many Responders think that a minor suit by Opener is asking for a major suit response. This is not true. Responder is expected to bid his cards as they are. If he is encouraged to avoid his natural "up-the-ladder" action, the result will in turn minimize Opener's chances to "see" partner's hand. However, a willful violation of the "up-the- ladder" principle might be done in only one circumstance.

Fifth, the avoidance of "up-the-ladder" actions occasionally makes Responder become the declarer when holding the weaker of the two hands. When this happens, the stronger hand becomes the "dummy". This certainly offers the defense a much easier task when determining what tricks are theirs and how to take them.

Sixth, after a one no-trump (forcing) response, Opener must often rebid a three-card suit. This encourages partner to doubt whether the suit actually exists. It also precludes Responder from ever playing at a final contract of one no-trump.

Seventh, if the opponents play the contract and the Opener's partner is on lead, he is in doubt as to which suit should be led. This is a terrible penalty to pay.

Eighth, the extended use of the minor suit opening gives more freedom to the opposition, whereas, a major-suit opening has distinct pre-emptive value.

> *Therefore, it seems illogical and nonsensical to willfully distort the description of a bridge hand. When any effort to show partner your size and shape is subverted to bidding what you don't have, it must be counter-productive to the principles of bidding. It is unreasonable to use an opening-bid method that destroys the capability of making a convenient rebid, especially when the convenient rebid will convey accurate and necessary information to partner.*

It is most revealing that when average players are asked why they open a major only when holding five cards, most cannot give a logical answer except "that's the way I do it". Also, when asked about showing partner the size and shape of a hand, most are completely oblivious of the methods whereby this can be done.

Vast knowledge and thousands of hours of study and competitive experience separate the skillful tournament player from the millions who just play the game for fun. The efforts on these pages are meant to give those millions a helping hand without having the "experts," real or imagined, foist conventions, disjointed exceptions, and high-level expertise into their thoughts.

CHAPTER EIGHT

THE NO-TRUMP BIDDING STRUCTURE

Partnership bidding of no-trump hands represents the ideal venue in which the "Principle of Captaincy" is illustrated. If all bidding were as easy as no-trump bidding, fewer errors would be made in the effort to reach a correct contract.

When a player can describe his hand within narrow point-count limits, his partner can guide the pair to the correct final contract. This concept frequently eliminates one of the players from the "decision-making process" and substantially reduces the chances for error. The idea of getting one of the players "out of the decision-making process" is what makes no-trump bidding so accurate and so simple.

In natural bidding, an opening bid of "one" in a suit has a point-count range that is very wide. Although Opener's rebid often narrows that range into a three-point spread, nothing approximates the accuracy of a no-trump opening. The standard method, used by most bridge players, embraces the arithmetic that a minimum of thirteen points is necessary for an opening bid and hand-values are measured in three-point increments. It is accepted that the first "three-point" spread is 13-15, the next is 16-18, then 19-21 and so on. Some players vary their spreads by a point but this text will deal with them as noted above.

Opening One No-Trump Requirements

1. SIZE (count) — Opening 1NT indicates 16-18 High Card Points

2. SHAPE — The suit distribution is "balanced" which indicates that there is no singleton, no void, and not two doubletons.

4-3-3-3
4-4-3-2
5-3-3-2

3. STOPPERS — A "stopper" is a card, or a combination of cards, that will usually prohibit the opponents from winning all the tricks in that particular suit. When opening 1NT, you promise that you have at least <u>three</u> suits stopped.

The following hands illustrate each of the above requirements.

#63.
♠942
♥AQ7
♦KJT
♣AK95

#64.
♠K4
♥AQ75
♦KJT3
♣A95

#65.
♠94
♥AQ7
♦KJT
♣AK952

#63. This is the classic 4-3-3-3 distribution. It is called "flat" because there is only a single four-card suit which might possibly develop a long-card winner. Flat hands are generally less desirable than others and experienced players tend to devalue them. Three suits are well-stopped and the high-card value is 17.

#64. There are 17 H.C. points in this hand with all suits stopped. The 4-4-3-2 distribution is desirable as either or both of the suits may produce an extra trick. This is a perfect no-trump hand.

#65. This hand has 17 H.C. points with three suits stopped. The five-card suit may be beneficial in producing tricks. This "good" five-carder tends to increase the overall value of the hand.

The Stayman Convention

The Stayman Convention method of responding to opening no-trump bids is played universally. The method allows a partnership the option of playing a hand in no-trump or finding a major-suit fit if it exists and is desired. The pivotal factor when using this convention is that the **RESPONDER** is the Captain of the hand.

1. The Captain: Because Opener has limited his hand, the Responder TAKES CHARGE OF THE BIDDING. This is ideal, and as noted in the first paragraph of this chapter, is known as the "Captaincy Principle." Methods other than Stayman may be used to arrive at the desired final contract but the best is the **Stayman Convention.** This text will examine two forms of the Stayman Convention and another convention called **Jacoby Transfer Bids.** An understanding of these bids should substantially improve your effectiveness in no-trump bidding.

As an overview, when playing Stayman, the parameters of action by the Captain fall into point-count categories which are added to the opening bidder's 16-18 (adjusted by one point if necessary).

2. The Sign-off: With 0-7 points, the Captain rejects thoughts of playing in a game contract and concentrates on whether to allow partner to play at 1NT or to move out of no-trump into the "relative" security of a suit contract.

3. The Invitation: With a "good" 8 or a "bad" 9 points, Captain will try to reach a game contract. Getting to a game will depend on whether Opener has "maximum" values for his bid.

4. The Game: With 10 (good nine) or more points, Captain will take the partnership to game. Game can be reached by a direct bid to the final contract or by acquiring more information about the Opener's hand before deciding on the final bid.

THE SIGN-OFF, THE INVITATION, AND REACHING GAME FOLLOW IN DETAIL!

The Captain Says "No Game"

Because the 1NT bid limited Opener's hand, arithmetic indicates when game doesn't exist. The Captain knows this and can pass the 1NT bid or retreat to a SUIT contract. Either the "pass" or the "retreat" is a sign-off. It is Captain's way of saying "NO GAME" and informs Opener that the responding hand has no more than seven points. Three illustrations follow. You are the Responder (THE CAPTAIN) to partner's 1NT opening bid with these hands.

#66.	#67.	#68.
♠Q2	♠QJ9752	♠752
♥J73	♥5	♥Q4
♦9876	♦986	♦A98743
♣Q765	♣J82	♣42
Pass	Bid 2♠	Bid 2♦

With #66, you have very little strength but your shape supports being in no-trump. It might be enough to assist partner in taking seven tricks. If not, he's going to be defeated.

With #67, your hand is a terrible dummy for him. However, his hand will be a great dummy for you. So retreat to the safer contract of 2♠. Your chances of playing for five losers is much greater than his chances of playing for seven winners.

Example #68 is much the same as #67. The bid of 2♦ is the correct call but a variation of this bid will be learned later on. A retreat or sign-off cannot be made in the club suit at the two level, which will be fully explained.

The Captain Says "Maybe We Have Game"

The following hands illustrate when the Captain has enough strength for getting the partnership to game provided the Opener has maximum values for his bid. Opener's bid promised 16–18 points. Whether he had the minimum (16 or a bad 17) or the maximum (good 17 or 18) is the determining factor. All decision-making comes from the Captain and it is he and he alone who will provide the impetus necessary to reach game. The Opener goes along for the ride and does exactly what he is told to do by the Responder (Captain).

After an opening bid of 1NT, Responder raises to 2NT. That raise, which takes the partnership "one short of game," is an INVITATIONAL BID with this message:

"**MAYBE WE HAVE GAME.** I am the Captain and cannot quite bid it because my count is a little short. I order you to recount your hand. If your 1NT is minimum, pass this bid. If you are on the maximum, bid game in no-trump. Don't think, just add and act."

#69.		#70.	
Opener	Responder	Opener	Responder
♠KQ7	♠A42	♠KQ98	♠A42
♥AJ2	♥65	♥AJT	♥65
♦K743	♦J52	♦KT96	♦J42
♣A62	♣KT832	♣A9	♣KT832
1NT	2NT*	1NT	2NT*
Pass**		3NT***	

* The 2NT bid in both auctions orders Opener to recount his points and Pass with a minimum NT or bid game with a maximum NT.

** No problem with a happy Pass because the hand is a minimum. Holding the 4-3-3-3 distribution, which is a liability, and having no middle cards, this is what is meant by "a bad 17."

*** Wow! Here is a maximum with the best 17 in the world because of great middle cards and a fine 4-4-3-2 distribution.

The Captain Says "Absolutely a Game"

If and when the Captain has enough strength to be in game, he should get the partnership there forthwith. He should bid 3NT directly with any no-trump hand in which there are 10 (or a very good 9) points or more. Following are five examples of Responder's (Captain) hands in response to a 1NT opening. Bid 3NT in each case.

#71.	#72.	#73.	#74.	#75.
♠A42	♠AK2	♠A42	♠42	♠AK4
♥65	♥65	♥K65	♥65	♥AK4
♦J52	♦52	♦7654	♦764	♦5432
♣KQT83	♣KT8432	♣KJ9	♣AKQT82	♣432

#71 is a solid 10 H.C. points with a possible five tricks in the club suit.

#72 is much the same. The potential for club winners is great with a double entry to dummy with the ♠A and ♠K.

#73 is just plain power throughout the hand with a little help for everything and should serve partner well in his quest for nine tricks.

#74 is unbelievably good as a source of tricks. It represents greater trick production than most hands of greater strength.

#75 is brute strength. The concentration of power in the major suits indicates that partner has concentrations in the other suits. Making game should be easy. Don't be surprised if the long diamond is forged into a trick.

Some hands belong in the major suits rather than no-trump provided a fit of four opposite four, five opposite three, or six opposite two exists.

Seeking a Major Suit "Fit"

5. The Stayman 2♣ Bid: Since it is preferable to play at game in a major suit, the **STAYMAN CONVENTION** facilitates *finding* a major "fit" if it exists. Playing in a major-suit game is usually easier to handle and more rewarding in the scoring column than playing at 3NT. Taking advantage of distribution offers the opportunity for extra tricks in a trump suit. It was noted on page 75 that a sign-off bid cannot be made in the club suit at the two-level. The reason follows.

(A) The bid of 2♣ by responder (the Captain) is used as an artificial tool or gimmick to ask Opener the question, "Do you have a four-card major?" The use of this bid indicates that Captain has one or both of the majors in his own hand and is looking for a fit. <u>The sign-off in clubs is accomplished by bidding 3♣ directly.</u>

(B) The Opener, in answer to Captain's question, can answer with one of three bids.
a. 2♦ = I have no major suit to show.
b. 2♥ = I have a four-card heart suit; I do NOT have four spades.
c. 2♠ = I have a four-card spade suit; I MAY HAVE four hearts.

After the 2♣ bid is answered, the Captain will place the final contract directly in game if the combined strength warrants. If not, then he will **"invite"** in the manner described on page 75–76 under **MAYBE**. The four example hands which follow belong to the Captain and illustrate his actions after his 2♣ question has been answered.

#76.	#77.	#78.	#79.
♠K975	♠KJ75	♠KJ75	♠42
♥4	♥AQ62	♥2	♥Q962
♦AQJ83	♦42	♦AQ63	♦3
♣J95	♣432	♣9843	♣AKJT85

Opener	Captain	Opener	Captain	Opener	Captain	Opener	Captain
1NT	2♣	1NT	2♣	1NT	2♣	1NT	2♣
2♠	4♠	2♦	3NT	2♥	3NT	2♥	4♥

The bidding of each hand needs discussion because there are very important subtleties of which all players should be made aware.

#76 is simple and illustrates playing in the MAJORS, NO-TRUMP, AND MINORS in that order of preference. With 11 high-card points, Responder knew that only 4♠ or 3NT are the acceptable contracts. He bid 2♣ Stayman as an inquiry about the possible spade fit. When it was found, 4♠ was bid directly. If Opener answered either 2♦ or 2♥, Captain would have bid 3NT. There is absolutely no decision that has to be made by the Opener. In theory, he is "out of the hand." Opener is aware that Responder found what he wanted and has enough for game. He knows nothing else and furthermore, it's none of his business!

#77 is much the same. The inquiry was made in search of the major-suit fit. It doesn't exist, so the 3NT game is bid.

#78 follows the pattern. Responder has enough for game and seeks the major-suit fit on the way to 3NT.

#79 has terrific clubs which represent a ton of tricks in no-trump. But if a heart fit exists, the clubs can be used as a depository for Opener's "losers" after trumps are drawn. This example offers a subtle inference to which Opener is expected to react. Imagine Opener has both four-card majors and responds to the 2♣ asking bid with 2♠. The

Captain would bid 3NT because his major-suit interest is hearts and Opener bid "wrong." Knowing that the 2♣ bid asked for a major, Opener can **correct** the 3NT contract to 4♥.

6. Responder's "Force": When his 2♣ call has been answered, the Responder often needs more information about the Opening hand. He must have a method in which he can "force" Opener to bid again. The Stayman convention was originally devised so that if the Captain bids a new suit, it is a one-round force. This idea is called FORCING STAYMAN. It offers flexibility and it saves space when probing for more information. Hands #80, #81, and #82 can be handled with ease with the use of "Forcing Stayman." Some players prefer a variation called "Non-Forcing Stayman" in which the "force" is executed by a JUMP in a new suit.

#80.	#81.	#82.
♠KQ743	♠KQ743.	♠KQ743
♥AJ85	♥AJ8	♥KT94
♦42	♦A76	♦987
♣42	♣98	♣2

Opener	Captain	Opener	Captain	Opener	Captain
1NT	2♣	1NT	2♣	1NT	2♣
2♦	2♠*	2♥	2♠*	2♦	2♠*
??		??		??	

In each of the examples, the Stayman 2♣ bid asks for a major. It is answered and then the force is made.

In #80, the Captain is seeking a four-four heart fit if it exists. The 2♦ bid denies a major, so the *2♠ force is introduced. It shows <u>five</u> spades and demands that Opener raise with three-card support. It is effective because in response to the 2♠ force, Opener has five calls available to him to convey specific information to the Captain. (1) He bids 2NT with a doubleton spade and a minimum count. (2) He bids 3NT with a doubleton spade and a maximum count. (3) He raises to 3♠ with three-card support and a minimum. (4) He raises to 4♠ with three-card support and a maximum. (5) He also can cue-bid an Ace which would indicate a super maximum hand with <u>very good</u> three-card support. The information should enable the Captain to correctly gauge his subsequent action.

#81 is a hand that may be bid to a slam <u>provided</u> the Captain can gain pertinent information regarding the 1NT Opener. If Opener has only two spades, the slam is kaput, but with three spades and the right cards, a successful slam is very probable.

#82 offers the best of all worlds as the Captain can seek both the four-four fit in hearts or the five-three fit in spades. Not only that, but if Opener has minimum values, part score can be played at any of three contracts. If he has a maximum, one of the three contracts should offer a terrific chance for success.

In addition to Responder forcing <u>after</u> he has bid 2♣, and it has been answered, he can also execute a different "force" by an **immediate jump response** in a major. The bid is rarely used, but has merit when Responder has a good hand with slam possibilities. To consider a slam, Responder should have a good suit and another source of tricks. Opposite a 1NT opener, the jump response to 3♥ or 3♠ is a "force." Opener will bid 3NT with any doubleton in the suit but if he has three- or four-card support he <u>must</u> raise to the major-suit game with a minimum NT. However, if Opener has a maximum and a "fit," he <u>must</u> "cue-bid" his first available Ace. With this information, the

Captain will continue as he sees fit. The following two examples illustrate the jump response and the subsequent bidding.

#83.

♠K74	♠AQT95
♥AK98	♥432
♦KT93	♦AQ865
♣KJ	♣none

Opener	Responder
1NT	3♠
4♥(1)	6♠ (2)

#84.

♠Q9	♠2
♥A864	♥KQT75
♦KQ3	♣AJ85
♣AQ92	♣KJ3

Opener	Responder
1NT	3♥
4♣ (3)	4♦ (4)
5♦ (5)	6♥ (6)

In #83, after the 3♠ bid is made, (1) the 4♥ **CUE-BID** shows the heart Ace (first-round control) and denies either the club or diamond Ace. It is an acceptance of spades and a mild slam try and partner needs no more information. (2) He just bids the slam predicated on the "fit," the heart control and his second suit.

In #84, after the 3♥ try is made, (3) 4♣ **CUE-BID** shows the club Ace, denies the spade Ace, and is an acceptance of hearts. (4) Responder's 4♦ **CUE-BID** shows the diamond Ace and (5) 5♦ shows the King of that suit. The Captain has the necessary information so he just (6) bids the slam.

If the information concerning Aces had not been satisfactory, the partnership would have stopped short of the slam knowing that two losers were apparent.

7. **The Delayed Invitation:** After using the 2♣ bid, Responder can invite to game whenever he has 8 or 9 points and needs Opener to have a maximum. This is done by the "invitation" of bidding 2NT (one short of game) after a "wrong" response or by raising the major suit

response to the three-level (one short of game). **Once again, please re-read the text on page 75 and 76.** Examples of each "invitation" follow as #85 and #86.

#85.	#86.
♠42	♠KT75
♥KT73	♥KJ97
♦AJ75	♦J42
♣943	♣95

Opener	Captain	Opener	Captain
1NT	2♣	1NT	2♣
2♦	2NT*	2♥ or 2♠	3♥ or 3♠**

In #85, the Stayman call elicited no major fit so Responder bid only *2NT. This is invitational to 3NT if Opener has a maximum. Remember, the Captain would have bid 3NT if he had enough strength.

In #86, when the fit was found, the Captain would have bid game with enough value. His **3♥ or 3♠ raise is an invitation indicating that Opener should accept with a maximum or pass with a minimum.

More of the Stayman Convention

The majority of today's players use Non-forcing Stayman. This doesn't alter the Concept of Captaincy, Sign-offs, Invitations, or Game bids. Only the **Responder's Force** via the introduction of a new suit, which was thoroughly discussed and illustrated as item **#6** on page 80, is eliminated. With example hands #80, #81, and #82 on that page, after the 2♣ bid was answered, the Captain must JUMP to 3♠ to force partner to bid again. Note the following auctions, which do not apply to particular example hands:

Opener	Responder	Opener	Responder
1NT	2♣	1NT	2♣
2♦	**2♥**	2♥	**2♠**

In both examples, the second bid by Responder who is Captain is underlined and in bold type. They both indicate a five-card suit (maybe six). If your partnership agreement is to play "Forcing" Stayman, then neither bid can be passed. If you are playing "Non-Forcing" Stayman, the bid should terminate the auction. A thorough knowledge of the structure of Stayman is essential in order to make a sound judgement regarding the method of handling no-trump hands that is best for you. As your understanding becomes more profound, you may wish to employ a little more sophistication in your no-trump structure. Get ready, because there's more to come...

Options and "Old Wives' Tales"

Regarding the Sign-off on page 74 and at the top of page 75, many partnerships alter their bidding structure for the minor suit sign-off. It is common, when using alternate methods of handling no-trump hands, to use the immediate jump to three of the minor as the sign-off in clubs or diamonds. Your opponents should always be apprised of which no-trump structure and sign-off method you use.

An old wives' tale which should be put to rest as soon as possible is the notion that the Captain must have an agreed minimum number of points before he can use the Stayman convention. Hogwash! Did you forget that a good and effective Captain keeps the Opener out of the decision-making process? Imagine that partner opened the bidding 1NT when you were dealt the following hand as Responder and Captain of the ship.

♠9642　♥J852　♦9765　♣2

It is an absolute certainty that partner is going to hell on a toboggan if you allow him to play at 1NT. Only a cruel or an ignorant partner would allow this to happen. Try to save him by bidding 2♣ Stayman. He has to answer in either spades, hearts, or diamonds which you will PASS. You can wager the family jewels that whichever contract he plays, he can be no worse off than he was at no-trump. Maybe you saved his life.

The presentation of the no-trump bidding structure is quite complete. Although there are variations and gimmicky additions, they offer little value to the majority of players. It is in the reader's best interest, however, to become acquainted with **TRANSFER BIDS** which can be very effective as an addition to your Stayman method.

Jacoby Transfer Bids

The Jacoby Transfer concept was developed by the late Oswald Jacoby as a method which would improve partnership efficiency when bidding as Responder to opening No-Trump hands. It is known that certain hands play better from one side of the table than the other. Having an opponent's lead come UP TO any "tenace" holding is usually an advantage for the declarer. A <u>major</u> tenace is an AQ combination and a <u>minor</u> tenace is a KJ combination.

Other holdings which are similar to tenace positions (AJT, KT9, QJ9, AT9, AJ9) also benefit declarer when they are led UP TO. Understanding this and adding Jacoby Transfers to your Stayman method can be productive and can make you a better player. Because great effort is made to find a major suit contract when partner has opened 1NT, the Stayman Convention is universally used to find the four-four major suit-fit if it exists. If not, then the five-three fit is sought which the Stayman convention can take care of efficiently. However, the probe for the five-three and the six-two fits frequently allows the wrong hand to be declarer.

Mr. Jacoby solved this problem by devising the following method of bidding when responding to NT opening bids ONLY.

ATTENTION: The Jacoby transfer method does not *replace* the Stayman convention but is used in conjunction with Stayman.

Here we go! In response to partner's 1NT call...

1. The Stayman 2♣ bid is used by the Responder to ask whether the Opener has a four-card major. However, the normal sign-off responses of 2♦ and 2♥ **can no longer be used** when playing Jacoby Transfers.

2. When the Responder holds a five-card or six-card major suit, instead of bidding it as a sign-off and playing the contract, he bids the suit **DIRECTLY BENEATH** the one he has. This gimmick transfers the bidding of the "real" suit to the Opener. Once the transfer has been executed, the bidding may end or continue under the guidance of the Captain. Consider the following hand as yours after partner opens the bidding with 1NT.

This hand and the accompanying explanation reflects one of the most important concepts in the game of bridge. It is the CONCEPT OF PREDETERMINATION which was thoroughly discussed in "Building Blocks." Experienced players use the concept continually.

#87.

♠K92
♥A9842
♦73
♣K42

You know the hand belongs in game. If partner has three hearts, the contract should be 4♥. If not, play at 3NT. This is "pre-determined" by you. You bid 2♦, the bid which transfers to the heart suit. When partner obeyed your demand and bid hearts, he DIDN'T promise any more than two of them. You should now bid 3NT. This bid (3NT) says: "Thanks for bidding my five-card suit. We have enough strength for game. If you have a doubleton heart, this is the game. If you have three or four of the suit, bid the heart game."

If you held the same hand with the five-card suit being spades, as a response to 1NT you would bid 2♥ as a transfer to your spade suit and continue from there.

When playing Jacoby Transfers, in response to any NT opening bid, (1) the bid of 2♣ is Stayman, (2) the bid of 2♦ asks for the heart suit, and (3) the bid of 2♥ asks for the spade suit.

The point-count necessary to activate Jacoby is irrelevant as there is *no minimum required*. If Responder has a very bad hand and wishes to get out of no-trump into the relative safety of a suit, he can do so. If he has values which "might" be enough for game, he can suggest this to Opener. Opposite a 16–18 point opening no-trump bid, the Responder should get to game with 9 good points. If a partnership uses 15–17 points as its no-trump range, then Responder needs 10 to get to the game. One of the more important nuances of the Jacoby Transfer, or for that matter any other convention, are the inferences that a player MUST draw from the bidding in order to act correctly. The following three responding hands, all with a heart suit, illustrate this. Partner opens 1NT and you hold:

#88.	#89.	#90.
♠K92	♠K92	♠K92
♥A98742	♥A98742	♥A9872
♦3	♦3	♦743
♣K42	♣542	♣J4

With #88: Bid 2♦ transferring to hearts. Whether the no-trump range is 16–18 or 15–17, bid the game with your six-card suit and full values opposite at least a doubleton.

With #89: Bid 2♦ transferring to hearts. If the no-trump range is 16-18, bid the game. If the range is 15–17, raise to 3♥ which tells partner you hold six cards in the suit and need HIM to hold a MAXIMUM no-trump to get to game.

With #90: Bid 2♦ transferring to hearts. If the no-trump range is 16–18, bid 2NT. Partner must bid game if he is on a MAXIMUM. If he bids game, he should bid 3NT or 4♥ depending on how many hearts he has. If the range is 15–17, hand #90 poses a real dilemma.

For purposes of learning transfer bids, the no-trump range used here is 16–18.

When the Responder has two suits, he can convey that information to the Opener through the use of the transfer bids. The next example illustrates this and the explanation follows.

#91.

♠QT743	When partner opened 1NT, the bid of 2♥ is
♥4	correct to make the Opener bid 2♠.
♦Q3	Responder should call 3♣ at this point. The
♣AJ864	spade suit had already been shown through
	the transfer and the club suit is offered in
	order to complete the picture of the hand.

This bid is **GAME-FORCING**. Opener can now pinpoint his values and bid constructively knowing the approximate distribution of the Captain's hand. Imagine Opener with a doubleton King of spades and three hearts to the Jack. 5♣ might be a cold contract, while 3NT is doomed and 4♠ is a "miracle" waiting to happen. Conversely, if Opener has three spades, he would contract for the major suit game. With a doubleton spade and good coverage in hearts and diamonds, 3NT is the final contract despite the major-minor two-suiter.

With BOTH MAJORS, however, Captain has the option of using either plain old Stayman or Jacoby Transfers.

If you held:

#92.   ♠KJ984   ♥AJ742   ♦K2   ♣5

and partner opened 1NT, you could Stayman (2♣) to see if partner had four cards in either major. If he bid 2♦, your next bid is 2♠ or 3♠*. Partner will raise with three-card support. If he bids 3NT, you bid 4♥ as he *must* have three of that suit. Handling the above hand in that manner precludes getting the Opener to declare unless he has four cards in a major. Some players, with this example hand, will bid Jacoby 2♥ to execute the spade transfer and then bid 4♥ showing five cards in the heart suit. Opener will pass this bid only if he has more hearts than spades.

One might ask, "Why use Stayman with five-five in the majors one time and on another occasion use Jacoby?"

This answers itself in the opening paragraph regarding Jacoby Transfer Bids on page 85 with respect to which side of the table might be superior for purposes of declaring.

Critical to the proper use of Jacoby or any other conventional bid is the knowledge of WHEN TO USE IT. Playing Jacoby Transfers does not mean you MUST transfer whenever you have a five- or six-card major suit. In the previous example which has 12 points in high cards, the transfer is recommended. The next example also has 12 points in high cards.

#93.　♠KJ984　♥QT732　♦Q4　♣A

If partner opened 1NT, it might be advantageous to have this hand become the declarer IF there is a five-three fit. Having the lead come UP TO the Queens could prove beneficial so it is not necessary to use Jacoby with this hand. When using conventions, you should be aware that no method is perfect and therefore no method will work out favorably all the time.

* When playing "NON-FORCING STAYMAN," after 2♣ has been answered, the jump to 3♠ is necessary to force partner to bid again. Of course, this jump takes away a level of bidding that some players do not wish to give up. Those players use "FORCING STAYMAN." With this example, 2♠ would have been a force on Opener to bid again. You and your partner should decide which method is more comfortable to use and which method best serves your bidding style and objectives.

A more obvious example is the hand which follows. For example, if you held

#94.　♠Q4　♥AJ9872　♦Q72　♣Q4

It is crazy to have partner play this hand in a heart game when YOU can play it and have the lead come up to the Queens. Just bid 4♥ and stay with the percentages. The hand may produce an extra trick if it is played from your side of the table.

The use of Jacoby Transfers is extended much further

than presented here, but special note should be made of the following auctions.

Opener	Responder	Opener	Responder
1NT	2♥	1NT	2♦
3♠		3♥	

In both instances, the Responder transferred to a major suit and, while completing the transfer, Opener jumped. This shows a maximum opening count with **four** cards in the suit. Furthermore, Opener also suggests that he has a doubleton because, if he had a "flat" hand, some playing value is lost. There is another subtlety in the acceptance of the transfer which indicates more specific information about the Opener's hand.

Opener	Responder	Opener	Responder
1NT	2♥	1NT	2♦
2NT		2NT	

Again, Responder transferred, and in each instance Opener called NT. This is an acceptance of the transfer showing a maximum count with three card support.

Where did the sign-off bid in diamonds go to? This is what is lost when the partnership uses the diamond suit as a transfer to hearts. In today's bridge world, the majority of players who use transfers jump to 3♣ and/or 3♦ as an immediate sign-off as noted on page 78 (A) and again in the second paragraph on page 84.

CAUTION, PLEASE! The rest of the no-trump structure is unnecessary to learn at this time. Wait until you are well-rested and have assimilated what has been discussed up to now before you go on.

Minor Suit Transfers

Consistent with efforts to reach a superior final contract and to ensure that it is played from the "correct" side of the table, it is possible to extend the transfer procedure into the minor suits. It is not necessary to incorporate this into your bidding structure, but it can be helpful to understand the meanings of bids which may be used by the opponents. A brief and simple summary regarding minor suit transfers follows. It is more sophisticated and precise when you reach higher levels of Bridge, but what is shown here is the outline of the concept. Note: In advanced Bridge, this concept becomes more sophisticated and utilizes an additional method called pre-acceptance.

IF the Jacoby transfers are being used, there is no longer a natural meaning for the bid of 2♠ by the Responder. As long as it has been eliminated from use, it can be resurrected and employed with a new meaning. The Captain can readily use it to accomplish a transfer into the club suit by responding 2♠ to a 1NT opening bid. This <u>orders</u> Opener to bid 3♣.

The Captain can also accomplish a transfer into the diamond suit by responding 2NT to a 1NT opening bid. This <u>orders</u> Opener to bid 3♦.

#95.	#96.
♠972	♠863
♥8	♥7
♦K3	♦K98642
♣J976543	♣T82

Opener	Responder	Opener	Responder
1NT	2♠!	1NT	2NT

With #95, the transfer to clubs is done through the "artificial" 2♠ bid and in #96, the transfer to diamonds is executed through the "artificial" 2NT bid. Both examples illustrate bad hands and the desire for partner to play in a minor suit sign-off.

Notwithstanding that our goal is always to play in the MAJOR SUITS, NO-TRUMP, AND MINORS in that order of preference, there are some hands that might be re-routed from the direction of that concept. In rubber Bridge and/or in certain Team competitions, the premium on making a contract exceeds the importance of a "higher" score which is the thrust of duplicate play. Occasionally, a partnership will forgo the 3NT game for a minor suit game or even a slam with the same values. Hand #97 is an illustration of this concept. Both hands are shown with a full explanation of the bidding.

#97.

Opener	Responder
♠KJ86	♠4
♥A8	♥92
♦AJ3	♦KQ942
♣K932	♣AJT74

1NT	2♠ (1)
3♣ (2)	3♦ (3)
3♠ (4)	4♦ (5)
4♥ (6)	5♣ (7)
Maybe 6♣ ??	

The opening bid of 1NT is normal and the response of (1) 2♠ says, "I am transferring to clubs. Please bid the suit regardless of how many you have." (2) Clubs were bid as ordered. (3) "In addition to my club suit, I am showing you a diamond suit of four or five cards with good values in it and we are now in a game-forcing auction." (4) "If you are nervous about the NT game, I have good cards in spades."

(5) "Of course I am nervous and I have no help in hearts or I would bid 3NT instead of 4♦ which is now verified as a five-card suit. (6) I have the Ace of hearts. (7) Play game in clubs.

The Texas Convention

Many players use a variant of Jacoby transfer procedures at the four-level. With six-card or longer suits, Captain can make Opener declare the hand by bidding 4♥ as a transfer to spades and 4♦ as a transfer to hearts. Just as he did at the two-level, the Captain bids the suit **DIRECTLY BENEATH** the one he has. The following responding hands illustrate this conclusively.

#98.	#99.
♠J97642	♠Q76
♥A85	♥Q985432
♦4	♦A5
♣A32	♣2

With #98, having partner play at 4♠ after he opened 1NT is easily accomplished by bidding 4♥. This is the transfer. With #99, if you want partner to declare, the transfer to hearts is just as easily accomplished by bidding 4♦. Repeating!! Just as in the Jacoby Transfer bids, you bid the suit DIRECTLY BENEATH the one you want HIM to bid.

If this method is used by a partnership in conjunction with Jacoby, then we can change one auction to have a more specific meaning. Responder's hand #90 on page 88 is repeated here.

Responder's hand #90 on page 88

♠K92   ♥A98742   ♦3   ♣K42

With this hand, if the partnership were playing Texas with

Jacoby, it is correct to bid 4♦ rather than use the transfer of 2♦ and then jumping to game. Transferring to 4♦ gets you to game with no wasted motion. However, it also makes the 2♦ bid obsolete with a hand such as this in which you have enough for game and can hit the four-level directly.

Therefore, when using Jacoby Transfers AND the Texas convention, the "obsolete" two-level transfer followed by the JUMP to game shows a hand that is a "slam-try". The following hand certainly qualifies as one with which the "slam-try" should be made. When a slam-try is made in ANY auction, it is rejected by a simple rebid of the "agreed-on" suit. When a player accepts the try, he signifies it by cue-bidding his controls in a step-ladder fashion, UP THE LINE from the "agreed-on" suit.

#100.

Opener	Responder
♠A5	♠KJ9742
♥QJ93	♥42
♦KJ6	♦AQ8
♣AJ95	♣K6

The Bidding:

1NT	2♥ (transfer)
2♠ (obediently)	4♠ (slam try)
Pass (happily)	

Opener has a minimum no-trump without an encouraging spade "fit." If he had the AQ5 in spades, he would have both a maximum and a "fit." This would create an excitement to continue bidding in acceptance of the "try" but a good pair would avoid the slam after recognizing that they had two heart losers.

However, change Opener's hand so that it looks like this:

#101.
♠AQ5
♥K953
♦K2
♣AQ95

The "try" would be accepted. Whether or not the hand would produce twelve tricks is of no real importance, but the chances are very high that it would be successful.

South African Texas

This is a special method of transfer bidding at the four-level. Rather than using the red suits (diamonds and hearts) as transfers to hearts and spades respectively, this method uses the minor suits as transfers.

This was the <u>original</u> form of **TEXAS** as it was developed by David Carter of St. Louis. This version of transfers eliminates the use of the Gerber convention, and many players prefer it for psychological reasons. The jumps to 4♣ and/or 4♦ DO NOT sound natural therefore, a lapse of memory is less likely to occur. Occasionally, a jump to 4♥ in response to a 1NT opener has been passed because it "sounded" like a heart suit.

Look again at #98 and #99. If the partnership had been using the **SOUTH AFRICAN** transfers, 4♦ would be the bid on #98, and 4♣ would be the bid on #99.

If a partnership plans to use transfers at the four-level, it is strongly suggested that South African be used rather than Texas.

IN SUMMARY: The Jacoby, Texas, and South African Transfer bids can be used in response to 1NT opening bids, 2NT opening bids, and 2♣ opening bids with a 2NT rebid.

IMPORTANT! When a partnership is using a transfer method, it does not, repeat, **DOES NOT** mean that a transfer must be used. Hand #99 is a classic example in which the Captain might wish to play the hand from HIS SIDE of the table. Instead of transferring, he could start with 2♣ Stayman and, after the response, he could bid 4♥. Please return to page 85 and re-read the opening paragraph of Jacoby Transfers for reinforcement of this thought. **CAUTION!** There are hazards in the use of these or any other conventional bids.

(1) If either partner forgets a conventional bid at its moment of use, the hand is probably a disaster.
(2) The accidental misuse of a conventional bid can lead to the weakening of "partnership confidence".
(3) The use of any artificial bid causes the partnership to adjust other calls to compensate for the call that is "eliminated."
(4) The use of artificial calls offers the opponents an opportunity to take defensive actions which were not available to them under ordinary circumstances such as a "double" to direct the defense.

Defense Against a One No-Trump Opening Bid

There are six reasonable methods available which are designed to enable the defensive bidders to get into the auction after an opening NT bid has been made. However, there is NO unanimity regarding which is most effective. They are complex, can be confusing, and probably should be used only by better tournament players whose judgment and skills are generally superior. Perhaps the best choice of the six methods to use against no-trump openings is the **LANDY** convention. It is simple to learn, simple to use, and accomplishes just about everything a defensive bidder needs. Before the structure of Landy is developed, consider the following important aspects regarding defensive bidding after a no-trump opener.
1. It is a fact that ALL knowledgeable players fully understand the tremendous power of the spade suit. Because it is the

"ranking" suit, the pair that possesses it can compete against any other suit(s) <u>without</u> increasing the level of bidding.

2. It is a fact that, if the strength is relatively evenly divided between the partnerships, the partnership that has the spade suit usually "owns" the hand.

3. It is a fact that after an opening bid of 1NT, a defensive bidder is at "high risk" if he bids with a **mediocre** hand because:

    a. The no-trump partnership rates to have greater strength and therefore, the defensive bidder is exposed to a penalty double.

    b. If the no-trump partnership plays the hand, the defensive bidder may have given too much information to declarer about the distribution and placement of high cards. He may also have guided the declarer into a better contract than the one he would have chosen without interference.

Landy

The Landy Convention is used in both seats (second and fourth) against a no-trump opening of any strength.

That is:	1NT-"Action"	The defensive player acts in the <u>second</u> seat which is immediately after the opening bid.
Or:	1NT-Pass-Pass-"Action"	The defensive player acts in the <u>fourth</u> seat which is after the opening bid, followed by two passes.

When playing "LANDY," there are five "actions," each with a different meaning, that can be used. Each is described and shown with illustrations.

They are (1) the 2♣ <u>bid</u> which is artificial and asks partner to bid a major, (2) the <u>overcall</u> which is natural, (3) the <u>jump overcall</u> which is pre-emptive, (4) the <u>double</u> which is for penalties, and (5) the <u>two no-trump</u> bid which is the unusual no-trump asking for the minors.

1. 2♣ (artificial): This bid is a "take-out" for the majors and promises five cards in both spades and hearts with a decent hand. Occasionally, a five-four hand might be held but when this happens the four-card suit should be terrific as in #103.

<u>#102.</u>
♠KJT84
♥AQ987
♦K4
♣6

Opener	Defensive Bidder
1NT	2♣!

<u>#103.</u>
♠AKJT
♥KJ987
♦4
♣Q84

Opener	Defensive Bidder
1NT	2♣!

The 2♣ Landy bid is artificial and says nothing about the club suit. It simply asks partner to bid his longer major. Major-suit ownership is what makes the bid attractive. Partner's probable support for one of the majors may allow the defenders to become the declarers.

When responding to the artificial 2♣ bid, partner has many options. Of course, he will bid a major if at all possible, but he may choose to bid something else. If he held a fine six- or seven-card diamond suit with no more than a doubleton in a major, he is allowed to bid the minor.

The next three examples show simple responses to

William J. August

Landy. The hands are not the best but the kind that occur frequently when partner asks you to bid and you hold little strength. The bidding proceeds as follows:

1NT—2♣—Pass—??

<u>#104</u>.
??
♠962
♥54
♦Q32
♣KQ875

2♠

I like spades.

<u>#105</u>.
??
♠3
♥T632
♦QJ92
♣9752

2♥

I like hearts.

<u>#106</u>.
??
♠2
♥43
♦AJT9752
♣752

2♦

I like diamonds Ha Ha!

The responses to the 2♣ bid are natural in all three examples, showing the suit you possess. If Responder to the Landy bid has a <u>better</u> hand with equal length in the majors, he can show it and create a transfer by responding 2NT. If he has a <u>game-going</u> hand with equal length, he can indicate it by bidding 3♣. Both are shown in the following examples.

<u>#107</u>.
♠A62
♥K54
♦QT985
♣54

<u>2NT</u>
<u>You</u> pick a major.

<u>#108</u>.
♠Q632
♥AT62
♦AJ8
♣32

<u>3♣</u>
<u>You</u> pick a major and I am strong.

In addition, Responder can bid three of a major as an invitational bid or can bid four of a major if he has a play for ten tricks.

2. **Suit Overcall**: This bid is natural and has no meaning other than, "I have a good suit and a reasonable hand." After an opening 1NT bid, a defender should act as illustrated in the following examples. The overcall will almost always indicate a good six-card suit or more. Without good values, punishment by the opponents can be severe. After an opponent's 1NT opener, overcall as indicated with the following hands.

#109.	#110.	#111.
♠42	♠K64	♠A5
♥AQJ987	♥43	♥J85
♦KJ8	♦AKJ9765	♦3
♣95	♣8	♣KQJT965
2♥	2♦	3♣
Natural	Natural	Natural, 2♣ is Landy

3. **Jump Overcall**: The jump overcall describes a pre-emptive hand and a desire to interfere with the opponents. Always check the vulnerability before making a pre-emptive bid to maintain a measure of safety. After the opponent opens 1NT, bid as shown with these hands.

#112.	#113.
♠4	♠43
♥AQJ9872	♥43
♦876	♦AQJ98743
♣Q8	♣2
Bid 3♥ ! Safe enough	Bid 3♦! Also, safe enough

4. **Double**: In modern bridge the **double** is for penalties. In old-fashioned times, the double showed equivalent values. It usually shows a very good suit, and if the defender has to give up the lead before the entire suit can be cashed, other cards in the hand will regain the lead. If the desired penalty cannot be gained, the defender should **not double** even if he has a good hand. After an opening 1NT bid, you should act as shown with each of the following hands.

#114.	#115.	#116.	#117.
♠42	♠K2	♠K98742	♠A5
♥AKQT972	♥Q74	♥Q6	♥A4
♦43	♦KQJ843	♦K84	♦Q92
♣43	♣K9	♣Q5	♣AQJ982
Double	Double	Pass	Double

If they run from your double on #114, you can bid hearts without much fear. In hand #115, the double will win most often. If they escape, let them go. With #116, you have no action to take. Let the auction go and see what happens. #117 is a double. If they run out, you might still bid clubs at the three-level.

5. **Unusual No-trump:** This bid rarely occurs, but if it does, you should be prepared for the hand. It shows strength and minor-suit shape similar to what is needed to use Landy for the majors. The take-out will be at the three-level, so watch the vulnerability and have strength for defense so that if the opponents find their major-suit fit, they will have trouble making their contract.

#118.
♠72
♥J
♦AK973
♣AQJ98

Bid 2NT for the minors

#119.
♠K4
♥Q9
♦AQJ84
♣K975

Pass, you have no bid!

♦ ♣ ♥ ♠

It must be emphasized that whenever a player considers making any bid AFTER the opponents have started the auction with a strong no-trump bid, he should have adequate values to minimize the risks. If vulnerable against non-vulnerable opponents, the bidder should exercise extra care.

CHAPTER NINE

THE WEAK TWO-BID

The Weak Two-Bid is an opening bid of "two" in a suit (but not clubs) which offers a description of suit strength and length, defensive posture, and a measure of pre-emption against the opponents. It also establishes partner as Captain of the hand. The actual point-count of the hand can vary from six to twelve <u>high-card</u> points, but will most often be in the seven to eleven range.

1. <u>SUIT STRENGTH AND LENGTH</u>:

The suit which is opened as a Weak Two should be a six-carder (not seven and not five) which is reasonably strong (almost always) to very strong (rarely). How strong should the suit be? Although vulnerability and table position are sometimes considered (the requirements may be relaxed with a partner who has already passed), the "good" suit will normally contain three of the top five honors or two of the top five which are supplemented by "middle" cards such as 98, or 97. Good suits should look like the following.

1. AKJ762   2. AK9863.   3. KQJ653   4. KQT843
5. KJT943   6. AQ9764   7. AQJT86   8. QJT843

It is important that the suit be reasonably strong because partner will do everything he can to either get to game or add to the pre-emption if his hand warrants doing so. *The least of his worries should be the quality of your suit.*

2. <u>DEFENSIVE POSTURE</u>:

The defensive strength which is promised when using a Weak Two-Bid is one-and-a-half to two tricks. Partner will rely on this. If he takes action, it will be reasonable and not something that would court disaster. Defensive tricks are counted as follows: AK=2 Ace=1 KQ=1 AQ=1½ KJT=1 Kx=½. The defensive values in the hand are not necessarily restricted to being in the bid-suit although in some instances, there will be nothing on the "outside".

In the above examples, the defensive tricks for each of the eight suits are shown here. 2 2 1 1 1 1½ 1½ ½. (QJx is considered to be ½)

In examples 1, 2, 6, and 7, the suit and defensive requirements are fully met so no other high cards are needed in the rest of the hand. However, in examples 3, 4, 5, and 8, defensive values elsewhere are needed to complement the suit in order to have a disciplined opening Weak Two-Bid.

The Weak Two-Bid is a specialized bid showing some defensive values but fewer than most opening bids of "one" in a suit. As a suit gets longer, its defensive potential becomes less. Therefore, hands with great length and general weakness lend themselves to pre-emptive purposes. A reasonable rule of thumb regarding pre-emption is "the longer the suit, the higher the bid."

Pre-emptive bidding is used to make it difficult for the opponents to exchange information when it is supposed that they have the majority of strength on a given hand. It is reasonable that opponents will have more difficulty bidding over a 2♠ opening bid than over a 1♠ opening bid.

Defensive strength and length of suits indicate the difference between opening bids of "one," "two," and "three."

An opening Weak Two-Bid offers more pre-emption but less defense than an opening One-Bid. It also offers less pre-emption and more defense than an opening Three-Bid. A Three-Bid is one card longer than a Two-Bid and disciplined players tend to utilize the Culbertson rule of "2 and 3" as the guide for opening a Three-Bid.

For disciplined players, Culbertson's "rule" says that when not vulnerable, if partner has no help, the opponents should not be able to defeat you more than three tricks. If you are vulnerable, they should not be able to defeat you more than two tricks. In either instance, the projected maximum penalty is -500 points provided they double you for penalties. A further suggestion is that the tricks you take are in the suit bid, not on the outside.

Regarding potential defense, if an Ace–King headed a suit of four or five cards, it is very reasonable that two tricks could be won in that suit on defense. However, if the suit length were increased to six, seven, or even eight cards, the likelihood of taking tricks on defense diminish as the suit grows longer.

The distribution of the hand which qualifies as a Weak-Two should almost always be 6-3-2-2, 6-3-3-1, or 6-4-2-1. It is very important that the Weak Two Bidder maintain his discipline so that he will NOT HAVE either a void or a side five-card suit. It is also strongly suggested that when holding the 6-4-2-1 combination, the four-card side suit not be a major.

It is not etched in stone, but the opening 2♠ or 2♥ bid infers that support for the other major is probably lacking. It is senseless to pre-empt ourselves out of a major suit in which we might have a "fit." Therefore, it is debatable (and not recommended) whether to open 2♦ in first or second position when holding support for both majors such as:

♠KQ5 ♥972 ♦KQJ876 ♣4

However, if your partner dealt (which puts you in the <u>third</u> seat) and passed, you should consider opening a Weak Two with the above hand. You might also use the Weak Two (in third seat) with only a five-card suit provided it is very strong. This is a tactical bid and should be considered since partner's original pass indicated less than an opening bid. Therefore, there is little chance that he will do something foolish. The emphasis is on the very good suit.

Two hands with which you may open a "weak two" in <u>third</u> seat are:

#120.	#121.
♣KQJT2	♣AKQJ2
♥K8	♥76
♦J85	♦987
♣654	♣654

The discipline of the suit structure and the defensive posture are the factors which answer the question, "What is the advantage of playing Weak Two Opening Bids?" Part of the answer is predicated on the principle of "Captaincy." Once the bidding is opened with a Weak Two and partner becomes Captain, he knows (1) the type of hand you hold, (2) what card(s) might be necessary in your hand to reach a game, (3) the opening lead he should make if you become defenders, (4) whether to add pre-emption to the bidding, and (5) how to gauge defensive potential if he feels the opponents are bidding too high. If you were the dealer and NOT playing Weak Two-Bids and held

♣AKJ842 ♥42 ♦9843 ♣7,

you would Pass and feel terrible if the bidding went:

(You) South	West	North	East
Pass	1NT	Pass	3NT
All Pass			

If you were playing Weak Two-Bids and were able to open the bidding 2♠, the opponents might not have reached 3NT and even if they had, partner would have known to lead your suit.

Responding to a Weak Two-Bid

There are six (6) responses to an opening Weak Two-Bid and each will be discussed and illustrated.

1. PASS!

All responses to a Weak Two are predicated on **winners and losers** and have little bearing on actual point-count. Remember that Opener's average hand will be about nine points and will have a good suit. You SHOULD NOT CONSIDER BIDDING without support for his suit or a very strong suit of your own. Even with an abundance of count, it is almost a certainty that Responder should PASS with a singleton or void in Opener's suit and with no other suit in which to play.

#122.		#123.	
Opener	Responder	Opener	Responder
♠43	♠KJ52	♠73	♠96542
♥AKT982	♥3	♥AKT982	♥void
♦974	♦AK83	♦974	♦AK982
♣93	♣AJ65	♣93	♣AKQ
2♥	Pass	2♥	Pass

In each example, after the opening 2♥ bid, Responder has a very big "PASS" which is accompanied by a prayer that the opponents enter the bidding.

2. <u>**RAISE TO GAME!**</u> (EXPECTING TO MAKE)

With a doubleton in partner's suit, you may be able to generate enough winners for him if you hold about 15 high-card points. Two examples follow which take high priority in understanding winners and losers in response to a Weak Two-Bid. You are the Responder!

#124.		#125.	
Opener	Responder	Opener	Responder
♠43	♠A85	♠43	♠98652
♥AKT982	♥43	♥AKT982	♥43
♦974	♦AK83	♦974	♦AK6
♣93	♣AJ65	♣93	♣AKQ
2♥	4♥	2♥	4♥

Hand #124 is difficult for Responder. He has sixteen high-card points which will produce four winners as a dummy for partner's opening 2♥ bid. If partner's suit is solid, he can take six winners in hearts. If so, the game is assured.

Since it is more likely that Opener will take only five tricks in his suit, he will have to develop either an extra diamond or club trick successfully to bring home ten tricks. With the hand as it is, 3NT might be a better place in which to play the final contract provided the opponents don't lead a spade. Note that the actual points are hardly included in one's thinking and reasoning when working out the **losers** if played at 4♥ or **winners** if played at 3NT.

Hand #125 possesses the same number of points (16) as does #122 but in the calculation of **winners and losers**, 3NT should be rejected because the spade suit is wide open and partner also rates to lose a trick in his own suit before he can bring the rest of the suit home as winners. However, if partner is <u>short</u> in spades as he rates to be, the responding hand can take care of five losers from declarer's hand and the combined hands should lose at most three tricks at 4♥. Again, the actual points are not prominent in the reasoning process while considering what action to take, if any.

When holding good trump support, which is three or four pieces or a doubleton honor, vigorous action may be taken by the responder with fewer high-card points because of a projection of fewer losers. The next three responding hands each have a progressively smaller point count opposite opening Weak Two-Bids yet each has an excellent play for game.

#126.			#127.	
Opener	Responder		Opener	Responder
♠43	♠A5		♠43	♠975
♥KQ9872	♥T643		♥KQ9872	♥A63
♦K74	♦AQ832		♦54	♦A9832
♣93	♣AT		♣K32	♣AJ
2♥	4♥		2♥	4♥

#128.	
Opener	Responder
♠4	♠97653
♥KQ9872	♥A63
♦K65	♦A32
♣432	♣A5
2♥	4♥

Hand #126 has fourteen high-card points and four hearts for Responder. After an opening bid of 2♥, Responder should envision many hands in which a play for only three losers will develop. If Opener has very good hearts, he may be able to draw trumps and "establish" the diamonds in dummy for discards of other losers. If his hearts are not so great, as in the example, he will have an Ace or King in another suit which will either assist him in setting up the diamonds or will give him time to do so.

Hand #127 drops to thirteen high-card points but this time Responder has the heart Ace which must solidify the trump suit. The presence of this card guarantees that Opener has a feature on the outside. As bad as the example hand is, a successful club finesse allows ten tricks to come home. If the outside King were in diamonds, the hand would have a better chance to make.

Hand #128 has only twelve high-card points. Responder's great spade length almost assures very few spade losers in Opener's hand so, knowing the trumps are solid and that partner has an "outside" card, trying for the game cannot be a bad idea. What is very important is that the partnership must accept failure (being defeated) once in a while in order to appreciate the positive results of proper projection of losers.

Hopefully, you are reaching an understanding that points matter little in some bridge scenarios and matter greatly in others. Responder should not be restricted or limited from bidding because he has little point-count when, occasionally, he may wish to further Opener's pre-emptive effect while holding very few high-card points. This idea of "furthering Opener's pre-emption" is a "must" when Responder KNOWS that the opponents have a suit fit of their own.

FACT: WHEN YOU AND YOUR PARTNER HAVE A NINE-CARD FIT OR LONGER, THE OPPONENTS HAVE AT LEAST AN EIGHT-CARD FIT OF THEIR OWN IN ANOTHER SUIT.

When you, the Responder, contemplate raising partner's opening Weak Two-Bid, one of the most important factors to consider is that you know where your fit is and the opponents have yet to find theirs.

3. RAISE TO THREE OR MORE! (PRE-EMPTIVELY)

Opener	#129. Responder	#130. Responder	#131. Responder
♣4	♠KQ53	♠QJ92	♠9743
♥KQJ942	♥T53	♥T84	♥T8743
♦432	♦A765	♦AK8	♦A85
♣K86	♣43	♣QT7	♣9
2♥	3♥	3♥	4♥

Hand #129. The raise to 3♥ is suggested because Responder <u>knows</u> the opponents cannot be defeated if they come into the bidding at a low level. If he passes, they will compete at 2♠, 3♣, or 3♦, at which point Responder will now have to bid 3♥ rather than sell out and let them make a part score. By bidding immediately, he may take away (pre-empt) the opponents' room in which to make any bid.

Hand #130. This is similar to the previous example. You know partner should make his contract and in addition, you are almost positive you can defeat the opponents if they compete. If they bid against your 3♥ raise, you can double them at 3♠, 4♣, or 4♦ for penalties. If you fail to raise and they compete at a lower level, you would not be confident of a successful penalty double. A marvelous "tip from the top" is that whenever you can cause the opponents to make the final decision regarding any competitive bid, you have a definite advantage.

Hand #131. The bid of 4♥ (or even 5♥) is very much in order. You know the opponents have a "fit" and they certainly should make a game or a slam. Eliminate some of their bidding room and gladly take a lesser loss if they double you rather than find their correct place to play. In each of these three examples, you and partner have a nine-card "fit" so you know the opposition has a "fit" of their own in which to play any hand which they feel belongs to them.

After a single raise has been made, as in examples #129 and #130, the Opener is **NOT ALLOWED** to bid 4♥. Absolutely NEVER! This is true whenever any pre-emptive raise is made. The Captaincy Principle forbids the player, who has limited his hand and finished telling his story, from entering the auction another time.

4. <u>BIDDING A NEW SUIT!</u> (FORCING)

The introduction of a new suit in response to a Weak Two-Bid is forcing for one round. It is almost certain that the new suit is at least six cards long but it may be a very powerful five-carder. It is expected that Opener will show whatever values he has when answering the "force" which includes raising the Responder.

The Responder, who is the Captain, is looking for a proper final contract and needs specific information to assist him in bidding. When using a sound Weak Two-Bid structure, partner never has to be concerned whether the opening hand is good. Therefore, he only wants specific information. The primary information desired is whether there is three-card support for the "new suit."

#132.

Opener	Responder
♠762	♠AKQ984
♥52	♥A98
♦AKT743	♦85
♣Q8	♣92
2♦	2♠
3♠	4♠

#133.

Opener	Responder
♠3	♠AKQJ84
♥53	♥AJ9
♦AQ9873	♦42
♣KJ95	♣42
2♦	2♠
3♣	3NT

#134.

Opener	Responder
♠32	♠AKQ984
♥53	♥AJ9
♦AQJ873	♦42
♣JT9	♣42
2♦	2♠
3♦	P or 3♠

In example #132, the 2♠ force was raised showing three-card support. Knowing that there are probably no spade losers and the prospects for ten tricks are very good, the Captain bids game.

In #133, Opener showed his good club holding in response to the force which enabled Responder to try the 3NT game. The contract may be defeated but the cards warrant trying for game.

With #134, the force brings forth nothing but a <u>simple rebid</u> of the opening suit denying support for spades or anything on the "outside." Game is out of the question so Responder must decide whether to pass and let partner play 3♦, or play in his own suit.

Some players prefer to use the "new suit" as a non-forcing retreat action, but this doesn't make much sense. Invariably, when a Weak Two has been opened and Responder has little strength, the best action is to pass.

5. **BID 2NT!** (FORCING)

The 2NT response is artificial and <u>does not indicate a no-trump hand.</u> It is simply a *"force"* which asks Opener if he has an "outside feature" such as an Ace or a King. This use of an artificial bid asking for a feature is similar to a Stayman 2♣ response to a one no-trump opener which asks for a four-card major suit. The Responder acts as the Captain and asks his question for the purpose of obtaining additional information which may assist the partnership in arriving at a superior final contract.

When queried, the Opener (a) rebids his suit with no feature to show. However, he (b) bids his outside Ace or King naturally if he has it, or (c) bids no-trump if his feature is a solid suit with which he expects partner to "run" six winners at no-trump.

Following are six examples which illustrate the Principle of Captaincy and the winner/loser approach to Weak Two-Bids. In #135-138, the opening bid is 2♠. In #139, the opening bid is 2♦ and in #140, it is 2♥. You are the Responder! Cover the Opener's hand and the bidding, then reason out your action.

#135.

Opener	Responder
♠KQ9764	♠A82
♥43	♥7652
♦K63	♦AQ982
♣42	♣7
2♠	2NT
3♦	4♠

#136.

Opener	Responder
♠AQ9764	♠K82
♥43	♥AQT75
♦763	♦KJ2
♣K2	♣76
2♠	2NT
3♣	4♠

#137.

Opener	Responder
♠AKQT64	♠852
♥43	♥A752
♦432	♦A65
♣43	♣A65
2♠	2NT
3NT	Pass

On #135, Responder is looking at only ten high-card points and many losers. You <u>know</u> that Opener's best spade holding is the KQ. To satisfy the requirements for his two-bid, he must have an Ace or King on the outside. **IF** it is the ♦K, a play for only three losers is almost assured. Bid 2NT to ask for a feature and if he shows anything but the card you need, sign off at 3♠.

The above reasoning process is predicated on a Weak Two-Bid structure which is sound. If it is less-disciplined, then Responder has no foundation from which to work and his actions amount to nothing more than guesswork.

With #136, the 2NT force is needed even though Responder is aware that the opening bidder could have a very good suit with nothing on the outside. If so, the final contract would be 3♠ which might be defeated. However, if something exists on the outside, game should be attempted.

#137 is a classic for Responder with his three quick winners. He can picture 3NT rolling home with a good spade suit so he asks for a feature (praying that partner's suit might be solid) and his prayer is answered. With any other "feature," the part score of 3♠ would be bid.

#138.

Opener	Responder
♠AQT876	♠K52
♥8	♥A9765
♦965	♦3
♣K72	♣Q654
2♠	2NT
3♣	4♠

#139.

Opener	Responder
♠975	♠AQ
♥A2	♥T9765
♦KJT983	♦A762
♣42	♣A3
2♦	3NT

#140.

Opener	Responder
♠3	♠AK8742
♥AQT984	♥KJ7
♦985	♦432
♣Q76	♣9
2♥	2NT
3♥	Pass

With #138, Responder should visualize a play for game **IF** Opener has a club honor which would reduce the many club losers to something manageable. He concedes a diamond loser so if the clubs can be held to two losers, a play for game is reasonable. The key word is "reasonable." He may be defeated on this hand.

In #139, Responder's diamond holding should ensure six winners. His many heart cards should restrict the opponents from taking more than four in that suit. "Knowing" that partner has a card on the outside, the bid of 3NT is a winner for nine tricks.

With #140, Responder knows that, in order to bid a heart game, some diamond or club help is needed. This will give Opener time to establish dummy's spade suit on which to throw losers. The 2NT asking bid will get the necessary information and if nothing good happens, the final contract will be 3♥.

6. <u>BID 3NT</u> (END OF AUCTION)

This bid re-enforces Captaincy. Opener has described his hand. Responder, with two methods available to force opener to bid again, disdains both. He places the final contract as in example #139 above. He needs no information, doesn't want to give the opponents any, and certainly knows what the final contract should be. This is hardly different from the following two hands, the first of which is almost certain to make, and the second one just a pre-emptive gamble on a prayer.

#141.		#142.	
Opener	Responder	Opener	Responder
♠4	♠K52	♠43	♠Q98
♥AQJ986	♥3	♥432	♥A5
♦85	♦AKQJ972	♦AQJ765	♦4
♣9642	♣A3	♣54	♣AKQT986
2♥	3NT	2♦	3NT

Nine tricks are there for the easy game in #141 and it looks like a certain defeat of 3NT on #142 if a spade is led. Who knows? The lead might be a heart and it is possible that a spade trick might be in order if the Ace and King are in the same hand. If doubled, a safe run-out to 4♣ can be made.

CHAPTER TEN

THE STRONG 2 CLUB OPENING BID

In the opening paragraph on page 104, it was stated that the Weak Two-Bid applied to any suit but clubs. The opening bid of Two Clubs is the only strong _forcing_, opening bid. It is **ARTIFICIAL** and is used to describe any strong hand which meets the criteria of what a strong opening two-bid should be.

After opening the bidding with Two Clubs, the Opener will name his "real" suit or no-trump when he rebids. In "old-fashioned" bridge, when using natural Strong Two-Bids, the response of 2NT is a "negative response" which indicates poor values. In modern bridge, the Two Club (2♣) opening is a catch-all for all powerful hands and the "negative" response is Two Diamonds (2♦). Any other response is considered to be "positive" and both responses will be discussed in detail.

It should be noted that in some instances, using the 2♦ NEGATIVE response can become awkward. Therefore, it (the 2♦ response) has been modified and refined to eliminate bidding problems. The modification is termed "2♦ WAITING" and is controlled and easily managed by use of a "DOUBLE NEGATIVE" which will be fully explained.

One of the advantages of the modern approach of Opening 2♣ as a powerful bid is that the most effective use of the bid is attained when playing it as a **force to 2NT, 3 of a major, or 4 of a minor** rather than a force to game. This doesn't preclude getting to game on all hands that warrant being there. It just adds a dimension to the powerful bidding sequences that didn't exist in old-fashioned bidding when one had to wait for huge hands that were dealt very rarely.

An additional bonus of this modern philosophy is that many hands can be opened 2♣ that previously were borderline and were opened with a one-bid. If you held the following combination as an opening bidder, what would you bid?

#143.   ♠AKJT96   ♥AK98   ♦A5   ♣6

It would be dangerous to open 2♠ (forcing to game) as in old-fashioned bidding, because you might find partner with a bust.

Therefore, you would have to open 1♠ and risk being passed out when partner might have any number of hands, such as the two examples which follow, with which game might be reached and made.

(a)   ♠5   ♥Q7632   ♦Q74   ♣9875

or

(b)   ♠Q432   ♥3   ♦7642   ♣5432

If playing the 2♣ opening bid as a force to **3 of a major**, #143 could be opened 2♣ without fear, knowing that the auction can be stopped short of game.

The following examples are opening 2♣ bids and regardless of partner's response, Opener makes a natural rebid.

#144.		#145.		#146.	
♠AKQ973	?	♠42	?	♠AQJ	?
♥AQJ		♥KQJ9765		♥A7	
♦AK		♦AQ		♦AKQ9765	
♣63		♣AK		♣8	
2♣	?	2♣	?	2♣	?
2♠		2♥		3♦	

In each of the three examples, the opening bid is 2♣ and after partner's unspecified response, the natural suit-bid is made. Imagine that in each hand, Responder has very little strength and bids 2♦ negative. Each of Opener's rebids are in bold type. However, if playing Strong Two-Bids with 2NT as the negative response, the rebid on both #144 and #145 would be at the three-level which loses a valuable level of bidding room. This (saving bidding room) is another of the advantages of using the 2♣ opening bid to cover all strong hands. In hand #146, if the suit were clubs, then the rebid would be 3♣.

The Positive Response

It is generally accepted that a positive response to a strong 2♣ opening bid should indicate at least a trick-and-a-half and a decent five-card suit. That is, an Ace and a King or, in some instances, an Ace-Queen combination. This requirement may be waived if Responder has two good suits (#149).

When a positive response is given, always attempt to make it the most accurate reflection of the hand possible. A positive response is made in any of the four suits or in two or three no-trump. Of course, each response should indicate Responder's shape. The following examples illustrate simple positive responses.

#147.		#148.		#149.	
Opener	Resp.	Opener	Resp.	Opener	Resp.
	♠A3		♠54		♠2
	♥QJT54		♥AKT87		♥KJ986
	♦J98		♦8653		♦KJ762
	♣984		♣52		♣52
2♣	2♥	2♣	2♥	2♣	2♥

#150.		#151.		#152.	
Opener	Resp.	Opener	Resp.	Opener	Resp.
	♠7		♠963		♠Q4
	♥K63		♥8		♥K98
	♦Q642		♦AQT752		♦JT73
	♣KQT93		♣QJ4		♣KJ98
2♣	3♣	2♣	3♦	2♣	2NT

In each example, the responder made a positive response which shows values and reflects the shape of the hand. Each suit mentioned has good cards and #152 reflects exactly what he holds—a no-trump shape hand with moderate values. In #151, it is necessary to bid 3♦ because the 2♦ response is used as a negative or "waiting" bid, fully described on the next page. Two good suits warrant #149 to be positive.

Any positive response creates an instant adjustment on the conceptual thinking of the partnership. First, a GAME FORCE is now in effect and second, a TRY FOR SLAM will be initiated **IF** a fit is found. It is usually best for the partnership to start its slam tries (cue-bidding) below or at the level of game. This allows greater latitude in which to exchange pertinent information and retains the Blackwood Convention in reserve to be used later if desired.

Two other positive responses can be made which have a special meaning. The first is the jump to three of a major and the second is the jump to four of any suit.

In response to a 2♣ opening bid, a jump to 3♥ or 3♠ indicates the possession of a six-card suit in which there is only one loser. This "almost runnable" suit would look like AQJT83, AKJT32, or KQJT32.

In response to a 2♣ opening bid, the jump to 4♣, 4♦, 4♥, or 4♠ indicates the possession of a solid suit which will almost always be at least six cards long.

This is definitely a "runnable" suit and will be AKQJT, AKQJ82, or AKQT862. The first is only five cards but should be included in the examples.

The Negative (Waiting) Response and the Double Negative

When responding to an opening 2♣ bid, the only natural response available other than those which are positive is the bid of 2♦. Therefore, the 2♦ bid can have two meanings. The first meaning is a simple interpretation that the hand is bad. A bad hand is one with less than a trick-and-a-half or, zero to seven points. The second meaning is that the hand *might* have fair to positive values but could not be accurately described. Following are six Responding hands to a 2♣ opening bid and with each hand, the correct bid is 2♦.

#153.	#154.	#155.	#156.	#157.	#158.
♠842	♠J842	♠987432	♠K6	♠2	♠KT43
♥743	♥97432	♥432	♥97432	♥Q9765	♥642
♦T865	♦65	♦Q52	♦852	♦K86	♦AJ42
♣965	♣J6	♣2	♣JT9	♣Q976	♣42
2♦	2♦	2♦	2♦	2♦	2♦

#153 has zero points, #154 has two points and #155 has two points. They are all bad hands. #156 has four points, #157 has seven points and #158 has eight points. A big question is raised! If the same bid is made with all six hands, how can one differentiate the hands with *no* values from the hands with *some* values? The answer is in the use of the **DOUBLE NEGATIVE**. This conventional bid is designed to clarify which hand is which and is easy to learn.

Explanation of the **DOUBLE NEGATIVE**: (only for Responder to a 2♣ opener).

WITH A BAD HAND...After the 2♦ response to an opening 2♣ bid, the Opener will make his natural rebid. If it is in a suit, RESPONDER will then rebid his cheapest minor which indicates that he truly has a negative response.

WITH A REASONABLE TO GOOD HAND...After the 2♦ response to an opening 2♣ bid, the Opener will again make his natural rebid. If it is in a suit, RESPONDER must bid something other than his cheapest minor which indicates the possession of values and a game-force goes into effect. If he bids a major, it should contain five cards or more.

Understanding the philosophical concept of the 2♣ opening bid with its responses and rebids should enable any partnership to become proficient when handling the many hands in this powerful venue. The chart which follows is a summary of Responder's actions with explanations.

Opener	Responder	Meaning and Interpretation
2♣	2♦	Waiting...could be <u>positive</u> without being able to make an accurate bid. Could also be <u>negative.</u>
	2♥, 2♠,3♣,3♦	<u>Positive</u>...At least 7 high-card points or a trick-and-a-half. A good suit of five or more cards. Game promised and slam possible.
	2NT	<u>Positive</u>... Balanced hand with 7–10 high-card points. It is *suggested* that <u>no</u> four-card major is in the hand.
	3♥ or 3♠	<u>Positive</u>...A six- or seven-card powerful suit missing only the Ace, King, or Queen. (KQJ1072) (AQJ976) (AKJ1082)
	3NT	<u>Positive</u>...Partnership understanding that it can either be bigger (10-plus) than a 2NT response or can show a solid suit. The latter is rarely used.
	4♣,4♦,4♥,4♠	<u>Positive</u>...A solid six or seven-card suit. Slam is almost a certainty and will probably be bid in that suit.

Powerful No-Trump Opening Bids

One of the greatest benefits of the modern two-bid structure is the narrowing of the point-count ranges of powerful no-trump bidding. In the past, there were three-point ranges to opening bids of 2NT and 3NT. A problem always occurred regarding the 22-point hand and proper evaluation of a Queen or King was difficult when responding to it. A most important tip regarding point-count for any no-trump opening bid is that which follows.

WHEN OPENING ANY NO-TRUMP HAND, SUBTRACT ONE POINT FROM THE HAND IN WHICH THE DISTRIBUTION IS 4-3-3-3 AND ONE POINT FROM THE HAND WHICH IS ACELESS!

If one were to consider opening the bidding 2NT, which is the most sensitive of opening bids, check your distribution and your aces according to the tip shown above. The no-trump opening bids are graded upward from the point at which a partnership plays its opening one no-trump bid. An opening bid of one in a suit followed by a rebid of 2NT shows a hand that is a little bigger than a one no-trump opener. Whether a partnership uses 16–18 or 15–17 as its no-trump range is immaterial. When playing the modern two-bid concept, the following applies.

Open **2NT**....shows	**21-22 high-card points**
Open **2♣**....rebid 2NT	**23-24 high-card points**
Open **3NT**....shows	**25-26 high-card points**
Open **2♣**....rebid 3NT	**27-28 high-card points**
Open **4NT**....shows	**29-30 high-card points**

When holding a good five-card suit with a powerful no-trump hand, it is usually wise to "upgrade" the hand by a point. This is consistent with the subtraction of a point when holding 4-3-3-3. Note that the two-point ranges which exist allow much easier and more accurate judgments to be made by the Responder who is Captain.

This chart of powerful no-trump bids combined with the 2♣ Forcing Concept allows the widest range of accurate bidding. Before showing several examples of the no-trump bidding venue, a conclusion should be drawn and understood regarding the general philosophy of 2♣ opening bids as it applies here and with hands such as #143 several pages back.

CONCLUSION: A **2♣** opening bid is a *force to game unless* (1) *Opener rebids* **2NT** *after a* **2♦** *response or* (2) *Opener rebids his* <u>original</u> *suit at the three-level after Responder has made a "double negative" rebid.*

The following are <u>Responding</u> hands and each will be analyzed twice—first, for a proper action opposite a 2NT opening bid and then a proper action opposite a 2♣ opening bid with a 2NT rebid. The Responder is the CAPTAIN!

#159.	#160.	#161.	#162.	#163.
♠974	♠K74	♠8742	♠A742	♠A742
♥8532	♥8532	♥8532	♥8532	♥KJ742
♦J863	♦J863	♦J8632	♦J8632	♦75
♣54	♣54	♣void	♣void	♣96

With hand #159, Pass the 2NT opener (21–22) and if partner opens 2♣, respond 2♦(negative or waiting) and pass the 2NT rebid (23–24).

With hand #160, respond 3♣ (Stayman) to the 2NT opener. If Opener rebids 3♦ or 3♠, bid 3NT. If he rebids 3♥, raise to 4♥. If he opens 2♣, respond 2♦ (negative or waiting) and after his 2NT rebid, bid 3♣ Stayman.

With hand #161, respond 3♣ Stayman to the 2NT opener and Pass whatever he bids. If he opens 2♣, respond 2♦ and after his 2NT rebid, use 3♣ Stayman and Pass. This action is reasonable and is usually successful.

With #162, you certainly want to be in game opposite both opening bids. Use Stayman for the possible major fit and if it isn't there, bid 3NT and take your chances with the void.

With hand #163, respond 3♣ Stayman to 2NT. If partner rebids 3♦, bid 3♥ which is forcing. Partner will raise with three cards or bid 3NT with a doubleton heart. If he bids 3♠, consider a slam. If playing Jacoby transfers, DO NOT transfer to hearts because a four-four spade fit might be missed. If the opening bid is 2♣, respond 2♥ and after a 2NT rebid, bid 3♠. If Opener has three hearts, he should indicate it and Responder would then explore a possible heart slam as his hand is worth more. If he raises spades, the same reasoning applies.

After any powerful no-trump opening bid, the Captain must do more than count his points. It is of the utmost importance that the point-count in Opener's hand is known so that an approximate level of bidding can be considered. The key is always trick production which is winners and losers. The next three hands are all slam hands opposite powerful no-trump opening bids. The questions are whether to play in a suit or no-trump and whether to try for a small slam or a grand slam.

What you will see may be very beneficial in slam bidding. Each is an opening bid, therefore the "count" makes it easy to assume slam. But is the count enough? Does the addition get us to the correct contract? It is easy when the Opener has 25 or 26 points, but does that mean we can't reach a grand slam if he has less?

#164.	#165.	#166.
♠KQJ962	♠AQ9642	♠A962
♥A9	♥K96	♥KQ96
♦Q432	♦K85	♦K83
♣4	♣3	♣42

With each of the hands above, a grand slam should be bid and made opposite all 25 point opening no-trump hands. Easy, isn't it? All that has to be determined is whether thirteen winners are there in no-trump OR no losers need be taken in a suit bid. That is enough for the thinking bridge player who works with winners and losers regardless of points, respects and accepts Captaincy, and has the ability to "work the problem."

#164 will produce a grand slam in no-trump if partner has *ONLY* 21 high-card points provided they are the correct ones. Try fitting the three missing Aces and the three missing Kings to the hand and count the winners. Beautiful, isn't it? BUT, if the 21 high-card points included the ♣AQJ instead of the ♣AK, six is cold and a finesse is needed to make seven.

#165 will produce a grand slam opposite 20 high-card points IF they are in the "right" places. How about the three Aces, two Kings, and any Queen? Even if the Opener's spade holding is a doubleton, the suit rates to run.

#166 is lacking a long suit that can produce extra winners. With two four-card majors, a possible major-suit slam is assured if a fit can be found. Match the following hands, (a) and (b), as the Opener to #166 and see what can be made. They each have 22 high-card points.

(a) ♠KQ   ♥A74   ♦AQ9   ♣AK875

(b) ♠KQ85   ♥A74   ♦AQ   ♣AK87

Both hands are opening 2NT bids and with hand (a) there are only eleven tricks to be had in no-trump UNLESS the heart suit breaks evenly. This is against the percentage. However, in hand (b), with the four-four spade fit for trumps AND the ♣KQ to make the suit solid, thirteen tricks are there provided the trumps are 3–2, which they rate to be.

This approach to winners and losers is the biggest factor in separating the pseudo-bridge players from the quality ones. If a player uses point-count only as a guide and emphasizes winners and losers, his ability is unlimited. If he lives and dies by point-count alone, he should play a game other than bridge.

CHAPTER ELEVEN

DEFENSIVE BIDDING

PART ONE: THE OVERCALL

Compared with the abundance of literature devoted to bidding systems and declarer's play, there are relatively few works on defensive bidding. Much of defensive bidding does not easily adapt to a structured point-count, so most writers and teachers offer only an overview of the subject. The reasons behind, and objectives of, defensive bidding are best understood when learned conceptually and philosophically. This understanding permits an insight into the nuances of competitive bidding that most players don't comprehend in a lifetime.

Defensive bidding is divided into three parts. Part one is THE OVERCALL and its RESPONSES. Part two is the TAKE-OUT DOUBLE and its RESPONSES. Part three is BALANCING and its RESPONSES. Although each part is a separate entity, a binding relationship exists between them. One thing is certain: if parts one and two are not understood, then part three will probably not be learned.

The philosophy of defensive bids is based on theory. In practice, theory often seems to contradict reality. The most severe test of a player's discipline occurs when the opponents open the bidding and thereby make the next player and his partner "defensive bidders." You will be tested often when theory and reality collide and seem to conflict.

The Overcall

Once the bidding has been opened, the next player and his partner become defensive bidders. The player immediately to the left of (after) the opening bidder is in the "overcall seat." Classifying him as a defensive bidder is a conclusion of simple arithmetic. If an opening bid averages 13 high-card points and the remaining points are divided equally between the other three players, the opener and his partner rate to have four points (an Ace) more than the opponents.

Percentages dictate that the pair with greater strength has the right to play the hand more often than not. Guess what! That means the other pair are probable defenders. While preparing to defend, one may bid a suit of his own in the "overcall seat," and it is that act which is addressed here for your edification.

All bridge books emphasize the point-count needed for different defensive bids, but most of the point-count requirements should be used only as guidelines.

Understanding concepts is more important. If you rely solely on point-count to overcall, you might find yourself in deep trouble. It would be advantageous to adjust your thinking to "good suits," "winners," and "losers." If the word "LOSERS" could be put into flashing neon lights on this page, it would be a blessing.

"LOSERS" is the single most important word in the study of overcalls. To counter the likelihood of too many "losers," it is important to hold a "good suit" which will produce "winners." This concept is the backbone to overcalls.

Good five-card suits: AQ982   KQT62   KJT92   AJ982

Good six-card suits: AQ7632   KQ7432   QJT432   AJ8732

Under normal conditions, a "good suit" will normally produce three or more winning tricks provided that suit becomes the trump suit. Each of the above examples will produce "winners."

1. Minimum Requirements for an Overcall

A. AT THE ONE-LEVEL: If not vulnerable, a <u>good</u> five-card suit is needed. If the suit is absolutely minimum in value, a King or Ace must be present in another suit. The "outside value" is unnecessary if the suit is very strong (headed by AK or AQ). If vulnerable, the hand should be about a trick stronger.

After the opponent opens with 1♦, overcall 1♥ with each of the following hands.

#167.	#168.	#169.	#170.
♠K8	♠42	♠A7	♠432
♥AQ982	♥KQT62	♥KJT92	♥QJT432
♦9732	♦K97	♦432	♦K5
♣AJ	♣432	♣AKJ	♣AQ

As a conclusion based on conceptual requirements, it is appropriate to place a point-count value on an overcall. The range goes from a minimum of eight or nine high-card points to about 17 high-card points. This DOES NOT give one a right to overcall because of point count. It only states that IF an overcall is made, the points will be evident as a coincidence. The ability to take tricks is far more important than the point count.

B. <u>AT THE TWO-LEVEL</u>: Opening bid values with a good suit or a hand that will "play as well" as an opening bid. Once again, the hand should produce "tricks." With the four previous examples, if the opponent opened 1♠, an overcall of 2♥ would be proper with the exception of example #168.

A player is usually wrong if he justifies making an overcall because he held "x" or "y" or "z" points. It is poor thinking to approach defensive bidding in such a manner. In the third paragraph of Part One, The Overcall, the reader was apprised of a possible conflict when trying to understand the overcall philosophically. If overcalls are made without exercising discipline in this very sensitive area, partner will have difficulty assessing his own values and reacting correctly.

It would be perfectly sound but terribly unrealistic to envision the foolproof overcall. An absurd but "ideal" example would contain a solid or semi-solid suit with enough length and outside Aces to prevent failure of the contract in the event partner possessed no helping cards. It would look something like this:

♠AKQJT9 ♥A4 ♦753 ♣97

Now, really! Expecting this hand (or one similar) before making an overcall is a fantasy and a player will age considerably while waiting for its arrival.

It is rare to experience the luxury of being dealt a solid suit and sufficient winners to assure success of any contract. Therefore, the theoretical approach to this portion of defensive bidding can be stated in the following manner.

> ***It is necessary to adopt an OVERCALL STRAT-EGY that minimizes the risk of failure of the contract while simultaneously not restricting us from entering an auction to compete for the right to declare the hand.*****

The most important factor needed to achieve these results is the quality of the suit. The better the suit in terms of high-card content, the better the overcall. Good suits have fewer losers in them—thus, fewer losers in the hand as a whole. The fewer the losers, the more the desire to advertise this matter to partner. And the fewer the losers, the less likelihood that the opponents are capable of defeating the contract.

These ideas cannot be overemphasized. The principle of sound overcalls reaps its finest reward not on the one-level, for few hands are played at a one-level contract, but on the battlefields of the two- and three-levels where both sides are contributing to the foray. While it may not be immediately apparent, a poor suit initially advanced as an overcall can lead the partnership to dire consequences. Escalation of the bidding through construction or competition will ultimately expose the danger of the ragged-suit overcall. Thus, to be fundamentally sound, it is necessary that the suit be good whenever the overcall is made within a minimum point-count range or with nondescript distribution.

After an opening bid of 1♣ by your right-hand opponent, hands #171, #172 and #173 are examples of good overcalls.

#171.	#172.	#173.
♠K6	♠KQJ92	♠85
♥743	♥43	♥KQT82
♦AQJ85	♦AQ8	♦KT8
♣853	♣K95	♣765
Bid 1♦	Bid 1♠	Bid 1♥

Note that the point count is incidental. Each overcall is sound because the suits are good enough and long enough to produce tricks. Compare the above examples with the next three in which exactly the same high cards have been repositioned and the suits have become fragmented.

#174.	#175.	#176.
♠K6	♠KT762	♠KT
♥A43	♥Q3	♥Q8532
♦J8542	♦AQ8	♦KT8
♣Q53	♣KJ5	♣765

These three hands have the specific high cards respectively as the previous three on which an overcall was made. However, the suits in #174 and #176 are so bad that an overcall is completely out of order. With #175, an overcall should be made because the "fair" quality of the suit is counter-balanced by extra-strong values.

There are other factors which may influence making an overcall despite the lack of quality top cards and internal strength. For instance, when a hand possesses exceptional distribution with 10 or more cards in two suits, it probably should be bid. As long as there is some high-card structure in the suits, constructive action can generally be undertaken and disaster will likely be avoided because partner rates to fit one of the suits.

There exists a great likelihood of finding the fit when holding distributional hands since the bidding is unlikely to die at the one-level.

This is more thoroughly discussed under "two-suited" overcalls.

#177.	#178.	#179.
♠QJ942	♠AJ762	♠97532
♥AJ985	♥4	♥65432
♦53	♦KQ964	♦AK
♣5	♣75	♣A
Overcall 1♠*	Overcall 1♠	Pass

When you overcall, ample high cards should exist in the suit which is bid. However, it should be noted at this time that there are special methods and "conventions" which have been "devised to handle certain" two-suited hands. DO NOT USE THEM! This in no way affects the concept of overcalling, and some exceptional situations will be addressed later.

There are, and will be, difficult hands to bid in a normal manner that may require the use of special means. Some of the more difficult hands (usually very strong ones) will be examined in the second part of defensive bidding, which is the study of TAKE-OUT DOUBLES.

*In hand #177, the overcall is suggested despite failing to have the security of a good suit. The bid is dictated by the overall playing value of the hand, so it might be necessary to overcall with less than a robust suit on hands similar to this.

Occasionally, failure to overcall creates the possibility that partner has too little shape or not enough value to re-open the bidding after two passes. (BALANCING, part three of defensive bidding.)

Yet, it might be "our" hand to play. Depending on vulnerability, defeating the opponents at their contract may not yield enough score to give us a good result. Thus, an overcall should be made at the one-level with these hands.

#180.	#181.	#182.	#183.
♠KT753	♠AT742	♠4	♠98
♥AQ4	♥63	♥KJ862	♥K86432
♦A7	♦KQ74	♦963	♦AK
♣J63	♣72	♣AQ52	♣K42
After 1♥	After 1♦	After 1♣	After 1♣ or 1♦
Overcall 1♠	Overcall 1♠	Overcall 1♥	Overcall 1♥

In each example, there is something to be desired in the quality of the suit. However, the overcaller holds cards in the opponent's suit which is advantageous in accepting the expected lead when declaring. If these hands are passed in the overcall seat, partner may not appreciate the need to re-open the bidding. Therefore, players who advocate overcalling with less than these examples, display, and try to compensate for, their glaring inability to pass now and climb back into the bidding later on when indicated. Again, BALANCING!

If we are "shut out" of many auctions, when it turns out that the hands really belong to us, it raises the specter of a lack of soundness in our defensive-bidding structure. Our less-experienced Aunt Bessie from Idaho may overcall with a poor hand and her venture may have gained a partial score. On the same hand, holding her cards, we may have defended and received a lesser result. Does that mean that our methods are flawed and should be scrutinized? NO! The discipline of not venturing into auctions on poor suits lessens, to an absolute minimum, the opportunities to incur penalties of 500, 800 and 1100 points. (Aunt Bessie gets them but generally forgets about those times.) The disciplined partnership, whose overcalls generally reflect a good suit, rarely suffers significant penalties.

There is a malady in bridge called "bidding with junk." Some highly skilled players open marginal hands with ragged suits and they overcall in much the same way. The reasoning behind "bidding with junk" is to confuse and take advantage of those players of lesser ability who, when interfered with, frequently don't bid their cards correctly. Also, lesser players rarely double for penalties. They are ill-equipped to take enough tricks to adequately punish those who venture into their territory. Learn to analyze and defend well, then cultivate an awareness of when the hand "belongs" to you and your partner. Be sound in structure so you can PUNISH THOSE WHO TRESPASS!

When average players adopt the "bid with junk" approach, they will ALWAYS lose and NEVER improve their skills to the point where they can be quality players. Measure your own ability by your minus scores against quality opposition.

2. The Meaning of an Overcall

A. "I SUGGEST WE PLAY IN THIS SUIT."

The overcall is NOT a method with which to show point-count, but an effort to send a clear message about a good suit and the possibility of playing the contract in that suit. In fact, you have probably put your "best foot forward" with the overcall. Without a good suit, you would pass and an alert partner who listens to the bidding will, in most instances, have a good idea about your point-count.

B. "I HAVE NOT ASKED YOU TO BID! "

"If you do, I will deem it to be constructive but not forcing." The overcall does not prohibit the partner from bidding another suit. Logic and reason should be the guide to whether another suit should be introduced. Assist partner in his suit if possible. Be aware that if you introduce a new suit, it may be passed.

C. "IF WE DEFEND, PLEASE LEAD THIS SUIT."

In most cases the suit which was bid is the suit with the highest concentration of power. Thus, it rates to be the best with which to start the defense. It is expected that you will lead the suit! Let's take tricks!

D. "MOST OFTEN, I HAVE TOLD MY STORY."

"Therefore, you are the captain and if we continue to bid, you must guide the way."

The overcall is usually a "one-shot" proposition. The player who overcalls plans to stay out of subsequent bidding more often than not. On arithmetic, he rates to have no more than his requirements, and if he told his story, what more can partner ask? If he has less than what is expected, trouble looms for this partnership.

Since bridge is the ultimate partnership game, you must always bid for the sole benefit of partner. This is done within a framework of concepts.

Be aware that if a hand is to be played in game, every effort should be made to play it in a MAJOR SUIT before NO-TRUMP which is before a MINOR SUIT as a poor third choice. Obviously, it is easier to take 10 tricks than 11 and the scoring table says it is easier to take 10 tricks in a trump suit than 9 tricks without. It is also incumbent on a partnership to know whether a hand "belongs" to them and if so, at what point.

With this in mind, it is easier to understand the philosophy of defensive bidding. Once again, look at hands #167 through #170 on page 134 and note that when an overcall is made, the emphasis is on the suit to be led and/or played. Each hand also suggests a deficiency in the other major, which is often the case. Think about the philosophy. If you look at hands #171 through #173 on page 136, the consistency of theory is evident. Each hand reflects the "meaning of an overcall" as to suit-suggestion and lead preference.

3. Responses to an Overcall

A. RAISE TO THE FULL LIMIT OF THE HAND.

When an overcall is raised directly, it should not be a

reflection of point-count. The level to which a raise is made is determined by a projection of "anticipated losers." Bridge philosophy and logic support the concept that almost all raises of overcalls are pre-emptive in nature. For a more detailed explanation, one can study this subject in the Encyclopedia of Bridge.

When declarer plays a contract in a trump suit, his focus should be on the number of combined losers in his hand and the dummy. Sometimes, a loser in one hand can be countered by a winning card in the opposite hand.

"Losers" are those cards which will be captured by the opponents' trick-taking power. Two hands are shown separately which illustrate recognizing and counting "losing" tricks. The first hand is "awful" and the second one is "great."

AWFUL	GREAT
♠7432	♠AKQJ
♥A872	♥KQJT9
♦42	♦3
♣432	♣A97

The AWFUL hand has 12 "losers." Each card, with the exception of the heart Ace, is a loser because it is expected that when played, it will easily be captured by a higher card from either of the opponents' hands.

The GREAT hand has only four "losers." They are, a heart card which will lose to the Ace, the small diamond, and the two small clubs. As separate entities, the two hands have a combined total of 16 losers.

However, imagine the two hands together as a partnership entity. If spades were the agreed trump suit, it is most probable that there are only two losers to be endured in the play of the hand. Of course, hands which reflect an example like this occur rarely but they illustrate the "loser" concept.

NOTE: When an overcall is made, the partner should "imagine" what that hand looks like and then match his cards to the image in an attempt to project "losers."

An opening bid of 1♦ has been made by your left-hand opponent, after which your partner overcalls 1♥. The next player passes. What do you bid with each of the following hands?

#184.	#185.	#186.
♠A9863	♠A96432	♠Q96432
♥974	♥974	♥K974
♦743	♦KQ9	♦2
♣K2	♣2	♣AJ
Bid 2♥	Bid 3♥	Bid 4♥
A simple raise is enough.	Who knows, for sure? It seems about right to estimate 4 losers.	Great distribution with no more than 3 probable losers.

B. BID A NEW SUIT.

Partner's overcall suggested a "place to play". Therefore, bidding a new suit implies that under normal circumstances, either your "place-to-play" is superior to partner's suit or you have an easy conversion from his minor to your major.

#187.

Open	Part.	Resp.	You
1♣	1♠	Pass	?

♠3
♥AJT
♦KQT982
♣QT7

Bid 2♦. This denies spade help, shows good cards, and is probably a six-card suit. Why else go from major to a minor and increase the level? It is non-forcing.

#189.

Open	Part.	Resp.	You
1♥	1♠	Pass	?

♠3
♥Q94
♦AJ73
♣AQ853

Pass this 13-point mess! Partner needs all you have to make his bid. If the opponents try a penalty double against him, a "run-out" might be considered.

#188.

Open	Part.	Resp.	You
1♥	2♦	2♥	?

♠AKJ983
♥Q94
♦QJ5
♣2

Bid 2♠. Partner has a good hand for a two-level over-call. You have no wasted cards and can possibly reach a spade game. Non-forcing but constructive.

#190.

Open	Part.	Resp.	You
1♥	2♦	2♥	?

♠AQ7
♥9742
♦4
♣AJ532

Pass. Say a prayer that partner doesn't bid again and that the opponents continue bidding. If you don't like the pass, try 3♣. The bidding implies that partner has a few clubs.

C. BID "NO-TRUMP."

Bidding no-trump in response to an overcall is a welcome option. Unfortunately, too few players either understand this bid or use it correctly.

The Bridge Encyclopedia states that bidding no-trump in response to a one-level overcall shows a hand of 9-12 high-card points. Be aware that partner did NOT ask you into the auction, so your bid must be constructive. More important than the number of points is the hand structure and the "stoppers" against the opponent's suit bid. Consider the make-up of the minimum values (nine points) for this bid.

It may be beneficial to your partnership and to your well-being if you transpose the nine(?) points into the values of an Ace, a King, and a Queen OR perhaps, three Kings. It is important that your points reflect good cards. This response indicates a hand structure which usually includes 1½ to two stoppers in the opponent's suit and "something" in the other suits. On occasion, only one stopper might be in evidence, but other factors may mandate the no-trump response to the overcall.

Your left-hand opponent opened the bidding 1♦ and your partner overcalled 1♠. What do you bid with each of the following hands?

#191.
♠72
♥K983
♦AJT
♣Q842

Bid 1NT
A classic hand for a classic bid.

#192.
♠A2
♥QJ4
♦K9872
♣JT9

Bid 1NT
Not a good hand for partner at 1♠ but playing at 1NT should be easy.

#193.
♠72
♥KT9
♦AJ9
♣KQJ93

Bid <u>2NT</u> or <u>3NT</u>

The vulnerability dictates which bid is chosen. If 2NT, partner will accept the invitational bid with anything extra.

#194.
♠72
♥A64
♦K9
♣AKQT73

Bid <u>3NT</u>

Sorry! You have one stopper, but look at the club suit. Nine tricks should be easy opposite any reasonable overcall.

D. <u>CUE-BID.</u>

Any bid of an opponent's suit is a cue-bid and, if used in response to an overcall, it shows a very good hand. This "power" bid is a one-round force which indicates an effort to reach game. It does NOT promise values in the opponent's suit. It asks partner to describe his hand more specifically, and allows great latitude in the decision-making process concerning the final contract. The one who overcalled can do many things. These hands illustrate the use of a cue-bid.

#195.	Opener	Partner	Respond	You
	1♦	1♠	Pass	?

You <u>must</u> bid 2♦, a cue-bid. Partner will react to the force by more fully describing his hand. If his overcall is the minimum that he promised, he will repeat his suit. With anything "extra," he will either jump in his suit or

♠K73
♥Q42
♦42
♣AKQT5

will bid his extra values. If, in the above example, he bid 2♠ in response to the "force," you can bid 3♠, which is your absolute limit. However, if partner either jumped or showed a feature in another suit, you would bid the spade game. If he bid no-trump to show that he had diamonds stopped, you should bid 3NT to take full advantage of your club tricks.

#196. Opener   Partner   Respond   You
        1♥   2♦   Pass   ?

You bid 2♥, a cue-bid. If you work at the table and think about winners and losers, you will conclude that your hand is not too attractive as a dummy if partner plays with diamonds as trumps. Your hand becomes super if partner has something in clubs because you then can play 3NT.

♠AQ4
♥KJ86
♦K1054
♣43

At this juncture, let's summarize and draw acceptable conclusions about the overcall.

Overcalls are defensive bids that highlight good suits. The temptation to make overcalls with poor suits should be resisted. It is an accepted fact that some experts and many pseudo-experts overcall with "junk" hands.

Some experts do it because it is part of a loose partnership style and/or because their superior playing ability enables them to take extra tricks. The pseudo-experts often do it to take advantage of weaker players. Players in this group cannot resist showing off. They never improve, they always give lessons, they always blame partner. It's a certainty that you know some of these players.

If you review hands #184 through #196 starting on page 143, a common theme exists. Based upon the overcaller having his minimum but sound values, partner is the CAPTAIN of every bidding sequence. The player who overcalls never acts again voluntarily once he has shown his values. The idea of who is the captain of a hand is another area of bridge which is relatively neglected in writings. Briefly, the player who first describes his hand releases captaincy to partner.

It is a fact that disciplined overcalls and their responses put restraints on "individuality" at the table. That is supposed to happen. When you study Part Three of defensive bidding, those who like to bid without restrictions will get many chances to bid with few cards. Please be patient until then.

The Jump Overcall

Bridge is ever-changing and new ideas are continually introduced which influence the structure of bidding. For years, the Jump Overcall showed a very strong hand with a long and strong suit. That idea became as extinct as the aardvark, and most of today's participants utilize either a "weak"- or an "intermediate"-type jump overcall. Both the Weak Jump Overcall (WJO) and the Intermediate Jump Overcall (IJO) will be presented in concept as well as content.

As background...It is essential that you (the reader) understand the structure, the use and the psychological impact of the Jump Overcall. Understanding the thought process behind bids and actions is extraordinarily important to becoming a competent player.

The presentation on jump overcalls which follows is structured. You will be impressed with good suits and firm defensive posture which is advocated by both the Kaplan/Sheinwold and Roth/Stone systems. They were presented to the bridge community in the late 1950s and both were influenced by the late Oswald Jacoby, who originally devised the methods in the mid-thirties.

Few players embraced or adopted the philosophy or use of Weak Jump Overcalls until the promulgation of these systems. Positive results were immediate. It was (and is) necessary only that the user maintain discipline and follow the guidelines of the bid for superior results.

One of the fascinations of bridge is the continual evolution of ideas and methods. The introduction and acceptance of Weak Jump Overcalls was overwhelming. Now, the use of the bid has become so commonplace that it is grafted into, and has become part of, what is commonly known as Standard American Bidding.

Be aware that some players intentionally and overtly alter the Weak Jump Overcall to their own taste and use. Some of them utilize a concept that eliminates the need for a good suit or any defensive posture. The reason for doing so is (in large part) an ego problem. Some of the players are expert but most are pseudo-experts who believe their natural and or developed skills warrant the use of any method to trounce less-skilled or newer players.

Since the majority of their opponents are inferior, those swinging wheeler-dealers take full advantage of the situation. They are quick to criticize and belittle others who attempt to improve through structured methods. The criticism is NOT justified. It indicates that the critic is usually (1) a fool who gets pleasure from trying to show how smart he is, or (2) an idiot who enjoys demeaning the efforts of those who are attempting to become better players. **These people are destructive to bridge!**

So remember! Assimilate the following information and try to refrain from taking liberties with the method. In the long run, discipline will serve you well!

The Weak (Pre-emptive) Jump Overcall

The Requirements:

1. A good six-card suit, usually headed by three of the five honor cards or two of the top three honor cards.

2. A mild defensive posture represented by $1\frac{1}{2}$ to 2

defensive tricks. A very good suit with 2 defensive tricks is usually too good for this bid.

When a hand has two defensive tricks and concentrated suit-strength, it is usually better to make a simple overcall. Example: ♠72 ♥KQJ987 ♦AT8 ♣98.

Quality high cards and disciplined suit length encourages the use of the bid without exposing the partnership to unacceptable losses. A hand in which a Weak Jump Overcall is used should produce 4½ to 5½ playing tricks. **Playing tricks are computed by adding quick tricks to long cards. A long card is any card <u>after</u> the third one in a suit.** This example, ♠AQ9872 ♥97 ♦942 ♣32, has only 4½ playing tricks and is barely acceptable. If the spades were better, such as AQJT32, the value is a half-trick greater. Noting this, it is apparent that vulnerability should be considered when making a WJO. As in simple overcalls, the risk of exposure to an opponent's penalty double should be kept at a minimum. You own each of the following three hands and are in the overcall seat. Your right-hand opponent (RHO) opens the bidding 1♦. What call do you make?

#<u>197</u>.	#<u>198</u>.	#<u>199</u>.
♠AQT972	♠75	♠64
♥42	♥62	♥AQJ972
♦63	♦A62	♦762
♣K32	♣KQJT65	♣43

With hand #197, if you are not vulnerable, this is nice Weak Jump Overcall of 2♠. However, if you ARE vulnerable, a simple 1♠ overcall is enough. If the partnership is not playing Weak Jump Overcalls, there is no alternative but to make the simple overcall. The reason for being affected by the vulnerability is the scoring table and the risk of severe punishment.

If the opponents have the balance of strength and double for penalties, a one-trick set is -200 points. If their balance of strength is substantial, they can choose whether to double OR bid game. The double is frequently superior. Risky pre-emptive bids expose a pair to a "fielder's choice." That is, if the hand belongs to the opponents, they have an option to bid game or part score or can forego either for a penalty double.

With #198, a situation similar to the previous one exists. Vulnerable, a 2♣ call is enough. The hand will play as well as an opening bid and it will produce six tricks if played. Non-vulnerable, however, 3♣ is a good bid. That's about the limit at which a penalty double can be tolerated.

When using these bids (Weak Jump Overcalls), it is expected that each hand will produce 1½ to 2 tricks on defense. This **"limited bid"** allows partner to be the **"Captain"** of the hand. If the bid accurately reflects the trick-taking power of the hand and partner has no useful cards, he (the captain) can often gauge whether the opponents can make a game or a slam. By calculating the score, the captain may consider bidding as a "sacrifice" in hopes of obtaining a lesser "minus" score.

With #199, the vulnerability factor is paramount. If vulnerable, a 2♥ bid is out of the question although some daring players might venture a very nervous 1♥ call. The temptation to bid should be resisted even if it is meant as a lead indicator. The hand lends itself to almost no defense and an abundance of potential trouble. If not vulnerable, a risky 2♥ bid is mandated. This is "thin ice."

The text and the hands which illustrate the Pre-emptive or Weak Jump Overcall will probably bring an inquisitive player to a question: "Why is this a good tool to use?" The answer is two-fold. First, when the Weak Jump Overcall is executed correctly, pre-emption is gained against the opponents. It is hoped that the pre-emption disrupts their "normal" bidding procedures and, despite their greater

strength, creates enough difficulty so they fail to reach
their correct contract.

Second, after the limited bid establishes partner as captain, he should be able to act wisely. He may determine to
bid a game. He may wish to add to the pre-emption to
make it even more difficult for the opponents. Or, he may
hold a reasonable hand with which to double the opponents at a certain juncture. Not only is he in a position to
determine what might be best for the partnership, but he
probably can set up the best defense as he "knows" partner's hand and probable distribution.

Another question should be asked: "Are there flaws in
this bid?"

Yes, and the answers are interesting. First, the Weak
Jump Overcall rarely impedes a **GOOD PAIR** from bidding their cards well and arriving at the correct contract.
Second, after arriving at the correct contract, the hand is
usually played in a superior manner because much of the
distribution and location of high cards has been revealed.
Third, if there is a choice of contracts, the pre-emptive bid
may assist the opponents in locating a superior contract
over an inferior one.

Considering both questions and their answers, Weak Jump
Overcalls are only as effective as the players who use them!

As mentioned earlier, bridge is not a constant. Therefore
it is only reasonable that if players were to utilize the Weak
Jump Overcall effectively, someone would devise a
method to parry this defensive thrust. It has been done!
Good pairs circumvent this defensive ploy with relative
ease. The method used is called the *"negative double."*
Perhaps it should be noted that the Weak Jump Overcall is
most effective against weaker opponents and not necessarily a tool that will strengthen your game. Good scores
gained against weak opponents can lull a player into
thinking that his game is far better than it actually is. A

strong suggestion to you, a student of the game, is to be aware of this dangerous pitfall.

With many examples of a <u>disciplined</u> Weak Jump Overcall, one could make a simple overcall. In fact, if one were not using this method (WJO), the example hands could be bid quite effectively. The use of this bid creates a problem of handling another type hand which occurs frequently. Suppose you hold the following example, and your right-hand opponent opens 1♦.

♠72   ♥AQJ643   ♦32   ♣AK3

You overcall 1♥. If the next player bids and your partner passes, the bidding may come back to you at the three-level and you are hard-pressed to pass. Actually, many players would bid a second time. The knowledge that justice was not served with the first bid makes it necessary to bid again. Because of partner's pass, that second bid is fraught with the danger of a penalty double. To be sure, harm does not come frequently, but this hand reflects a weakness of the WJO. This weakness might be avoided and is explained starting on page 155.

Responding to a Weak Jump Overcall

When responding to a Weak Jump Overcall, one should follow the same guidelines he would use when responding to a simple overcall.

Holding most weak hands <u>with</u> support for partner's suit, responder might raise for pre-emptive purposes and/or a possible sacrifice. Remember that when an overcall is made in which the story has been told, that player releases captaincy to his partner. If the captain has good cards, he can consider a defensive position provided the opponents continue to bid. He may also consider game and slam possibilities.

A cue-bid or another "forcing" bid may be used to make the overcaller bid again. In response to a Weak Jump Overcall, the bid of 2NT is commonly used as a force the same as it is used in response to a Weak-Two opening bid. It asks partner for added information but does not promise no-trump shape. Specifically, 2NT asks whether he has an outside "feature" (an Ace or a King). If there is no "feature," a simple rebid of the suit will indicate this.

#200.
North
♠92
♥KJT942
♦85
♣A73

South
♠QJT8
♥A83
♦KQ72
♣K9

#201.
North
♠92
♥AKQT92
♦85
♣873

South
♠KJT8
♥853
♦KQ9
♣AQT

West	North	East	South
1♦	2♥*	Pass	2NT#
Pass	3♣^	Pass	4♥

West	North	East	South
1♣	2♥*	Pass	2NT#
Pass	3NT^	(End)	

With #200, after an opening bid of 1♦ by West, your partner who is North bids 2♥*, which is a Weak Jump Overcall. East passes to you. Because you hold the Ace in his suit, you know that his very best heart holding includes the King and Queen.

Therefore, he must have an outside feature. If he has the diamond Ace, there could be two losing spades and two losing clubs. If he has the club Ace, there is a strong play for game with only two spades and one diamond as projected losers. Using this reasoning, the 2NT# bid asks for the feature, and when the club Ace is shown, game is bid.

In example #201, the 2♥* bid is made after the opening 1♣ bid. The 2NT bid asks for a feature if it exists and partner obligingly bids 3NT, which is the call to show the feature of a "running" suit which can be used in no-trump play.

The Intermediate (Good) Jump Overcall

This bid shows a hand with a good six- or seven-card suit and solid defensive posture. The strength of the hand is intermediate, that is, a "second bracket" hand. A second bracket hand is essentially 16–18 points, but many hands of 14–17 high-card points count to 16–18 when distributional values are included.

Many players who are NOT absolute point-counters use the playing-trick count for determining an Intermediate Jump Overcall. Any hand with a good six- or seven-card suit that counts to 6½ or 7 playing tricks qualifies for this bid. With a fine spade suit, the use of this bid is encouraged with only six playing tricks. For the players who need to be reminded, a full explanation of the method of counting playing tricks is given here.

Playing Trick Count

First, count the quick tricks in the hand. Then find the longest suit. Each card AFTER the third one in that suit is a long card (1 trick). If there is a second suit, each card AFTER the third one is one-half long card (½ trick). Add the quick tricks to the long cards and the half-long cards.

The sum is the number of playing tricks in the hand that coincides with the number of tricks the hand will produce if the long suit becomes the trump suit. Of course, under very adverse circumstances, some power will be negated, but the exception cannot be allowed to supersede the norm. The playing-trick method of evaluation is more accurate than the point-count method when establishing the worth of a hand.

After making an Intermediate Jump Overcall, captaincy is released to partner in the same manner as all other over-calls. Partner plans the strategy: bidding a game, sacrific-ing, attempting to play in no-trump, cue-bidding for added information, and/or setting a line of defense. The concept of captaincy can be fully exploited only when a partnership is structured and disciplined. It is in this very sensitive area that most players find themselves groping for the "correct" action after partner has made any type of overcall. The captain cannot be expected to do much that is "right" if his partner isn't considered reliable.

Weak and Intermediate Jump Overcalls cannot be played at the same time on the same hand. However, when a partnership decides to use Intermediate Jump Overcalls, hands that were previously bid by using a Weak Jump Overcall can usually be handled with a simple overcall.

Little is lost by NOT using Weak Jump Overcalls. A good and/or knowledgeable pair can blunt the effectiveness of the WJO with the convention devised for that purpose. It was mentioned earlier. The convention is called the "Negative Double."

Following are example hands that highlight the Intermediate Jump Overcall.

#202.

You hold: ♠AQJ974

♥Q3

♦72

♣AQ7

RHO opened the bidding with 1♠. What call do you make?

Bid 2♠! You have a good six-card suit and many points. Partner should envision your playing trick potential and will try for game if he can.

#203.

You hold: ♠4

♥A7

♦8743

♣AKQJ84

RHO opened the bidding with 1 ♠. What call do you make?

Bid 3♣! Perfect description of an Intermediate Jump Overcall. Hopefully, partner will have cards with which to bid 3NT. If he can, you will produce seven winners for him.

#204.

RHO opened 1♣. What do you bid with this hand?

♠432

♥AKT9643

♦A6

♣2

Bid 2♥! Despite having only 11 high-card points, the hand has seven playing tricks with hearts as trumps. This is the best bid to describe this hand to partner.

#205.

RHO opened 1♥. What do you bid with this hand?

♠K7

♥K2

♦AQT843

♣K94

Bid 3♦! This has to be the best possible bid for partner. Even though there are only six playing tricks, two of the kings should be "upgraded."

Study each of the four previous hands very carefully. If a simple overcall was made instead of a jump, there is no questioning that the bid is inadequate. Because of this, the opponents could easily be at the three-level when the bidding returns to you. Should you bid again? No problem exists if you had jumped immediately and gotten out of the way. You have a partner, you know.

Return to page 153 and look at the example hand in the middle of the page. The use of Weak Jump Overcalls prohibited a firm and accurate action with those cards. Examples like that influence some players to compromise in their use of Jump Overcalls.

Some world-class players use the Weak Jump Overcalls only when non-vulnerable, and Intermediate Jump Overcalls when vulnerable. This suggests that perhaps the reader should consider adopting the same philosophy. The following examples illustrate responding to a Jump Overcall with the same hand under both conditions—being **non-vulnerable** and being **vulnerable**.

#206.

Open	Part.	Resp.	**YOU**
1♥	2♠	4♥	?

♠9
♥Q972
♦KT93
♣Q742

#207.

Open	Part.	Resp.	**YOU**
1♥	3♦	Pass	?

♠AJ9
♥QT94
♦K6
♣QJ32

You **Pass** if not vulnerable. Partner bid a Weak Jump Overcall. If vulnerable, the bid was Intermediate and you must **Double** for penalties.

Pass not vulnerable. Bid **3NT** if vulnerable. Partner's different hands on the same auction dictate different actions by you.

#208.				#209.			
Open	Part.	Resp.	**YOU**	Open	Part.	Resp.	YOU
1♦	2♠	Pass	?	1♠	3♣	3♠	?

♠K2	♠QJ9
♥Q98	♥A6
♦764	♦QT8
♣AKJ92	♣97642

Pass non-vulnerable but compete to 3♠ if necessary. If vulnerable, bid **3♦**, a **cue-bid**! Hope that partner has a diamond stopper and bids 3NT. If not, play in 4♠.

Bid 5♣ not vulnerable. Game should be conceded to them. Be happy if they double 5♣, or let them play at 5♠. If vulnerable, bid **3NT**. A play for this game is more than reasonable.

The Two-suited Overcall

It is not uncommon that, after an opening bid, the next player could have a good hand with two suits to bid. This is one of the most awkward bidding situations in bridge. There are different opinions as to the most effective way to handle this problem, but "bidding naturally" is probably the very best for the majority of players. A phenomenon of "bidding naturally" sometimes forces the bidder to speculate how an auction will go and then insert his bids accordingly and in a manner that is economical. The plan is to bid twice!

When the two suits are either five or six cards long and adjacent to each other, it is almost always correct to overcall first with the *higher-ranking suit*. If partner raises it, your trump suit is established. If partner shows no interest, you may introduce the other (lower) suit at your next opportunity. This may necessitate introducing a five-card suit before a six-card suit to prohibit the partnership from being one level higher than desired (bidding economically).

Imagine that your RHO opens the bidding when you

hold two suits and a hand with good values. An overcall in one of the suits is made. Most of the time, the distribution of your hand plus the opening bid reflects acute distribution in at least one other hand. This factor almost always precludes the original overcall from being passed out. Therefore, it is almost a certainty that **someone** at the table will bid, which ensures your getting a chance to bid again. If not, c'est la vie!

Following are four examples. You are South. Cover the other hands and study the auctions. Insert your choice of bids where called for before looking at the explanations which start on the next page. East always deals.

#210.　North
　　　　♠82
　　　　♥43
　　　　♦A762
　　　　♣QJ865

West　　　　　East
♠KJ976　　　　♠AQT53
♥865　　　　　♥KQ9
♦3　　　　　　♦954
♣AT94　　　　♣K3

　　　　South
　　　　♠4
　　　　♥AJT72
　　　　♦KQJT8
　　　　♣72

East	South	West	North
1♠	2♥	4♠	Pass
Pass	?		

#211.　North
　　　　♠Q976
　　　　♥J76
　　　　♦J876
　　　　♣97

West　　　　　East
♠J53　　　　　♠2
♥AKQT9　　　♥8543
♦42　　　　　♦AQT95
♣654　　　　　♣AQ3

　　　　South
　　　　♠AKT84
　　　　♥2
　　　　♦K3
　　　　♣KJT82

East	South	West	North
1♦	2♣	2♥	Pass
4♥	?		

#212.　North
♠82
♥T876
♦K2
♣J9765

West
♠KT975
♥K2
♦53
♣AQT8

East
♠AQJ43
♥43
♦QJ7
♣K43

South
♠6
♥AQJ95
♦AT9864
♣2

#213.　North
♠542
♥2
♦653
♣QT8753

West
♠J7
♥K964
♦AJ9
♣A964

East
♠Q83
♥AQT85
♦Q2
♣KJ2

South
♠AKT96
♥J73
♦KT874
♣ void

East	South	West	North
1♠	2♥	3♠	Pass
4♠	?		

East	South	West	North
1♥	2♦	3♥	Pass
4♥	?		

You should bid 5♦ on hand #210. This completes the two-suited overcall with touching (adjacent) suits. West's call of 4♠ indicates a distributional hand without an abundance of high cards. Every time a pair has a nine-card suit or longer, the other pair MUST have an eight-card suit or longer. Therefore, "knowing" that a fit exists with your very good hand, you must bid to find it. The EW pair can make a game while NS goes down two. What will EW do? Will they defend or pursue to the unmakeable 5♠ contract?

With hand #211, you must bid 4♠. Not only do you have a very good hand, but a "fit" must exist. The original call of 2♣ was necessary so that if the opponents had a heart fit, you could bid spades economically. If spades were bid first, then over 4♥ you would have to bid clubs at the five-level. NS can make a game in spades. If EW play in hearts, they can make five without a club lead by North. If the opening lead is the ♣9, EW is down one at 4♥.

With hand #212, bid 5♦. Note the five-card heart suit was bid first for the sake of economy. North corrects the bid to 5♥ which gets beaten one trick. Conversely, EW had an easy game in spades. Once again, the "fit" was there and the EW pair had to guess whether to defend or bid and perhaps find themselves too high.

The last hand, #213, is bid similarly to #211. Diamonds had to be bid first so the bid of 4♠ could be made economically. If spades were bid first, the potential loss is too great to bid 5♦. The club void and three trumps may seem to be enough to cause trouble for EW. Actually, EW makes a lot in hearts and if South had overcalled with 1♠ and followed with 5♦, disaster would have occurred.

The One No-Trump Overcall

The exact point-count range of suit overcalls is difficult to ascertain. Minimum requirements can be judged, but the maximum values are vague. This is not so with the one no-trump overcall, which is a descriptive and limited bid. Bids such as this are desired because the parameters of count and shape are well defined and partner can manage accordingly.

The value needed for this bid is that of a strong 1NT opening; that is, 16–18 high-card points. Many players use 16–19, which has merit. Bidding 1NT as an overcall without solid values is dangerous because there is little strength remaining for the other players at the table. Too often, the value of dummy's few high cards is negated by the defender. This factor usually precludes "getting to the dummy" with ease. If the dummy can't be reached, tricks cannot be gained by means of playing through the original bidder.

Be aware of high-card placement and major-suit distribution of a 1NT overcall as opposed to a 1NT opener. In an opener, the high cards and stoppers are expected to be scattered throughout the hand. This is modified in an over-call. Because the "expected" lead is known, two stoppers in that suit are anticipated but not assured. Also, an opening 1NT bid may have two four-card majors.

After a NT overcall of a major-suit opening, the NT hand usually will not have four cards in the <u>other</u> major. With four cards in the other major, a take-out double is often the preferred defensive bid rather than the overcall. "Take-out doubles" are fully discussed in part two of defensive bidding, but in the hands which follow, it is necessary to show a differentiation between the two bids.

You hold the following hand on both #214 and #215. In the first example (#214), your RHO opens 1♦. What call do you make? In the second example (#215), your RHO opens 1♥. What call do you make?

♠KJ74
♥KT
♦AQ6
♣A975

#214. After a 1♦ opening, the most descriptive bid is <u>1NT</u>! This limits the hand for partner and protects the diamond holding. If you double, partner is more likely to bid hearts than spades. If he does this, this could be a problem because if you then bid no-trump, it would indicate a hand stronger than the example.

#215. After a 1♥ opening, <u>DOUBLE</u>! The single stopper in hearts influences the decision. It is a more disciplined action than a 1NT bid and begs partner to bid spades. Raise partner's spade response but pass any other simple response. Go to game opposite any aggressive action by partner. Game may be defeated, but you win some and you lose some. Next deal!

When bidding defensively, it is often difficult to choose which of two actions is superior. With any given hand, a double might be better than an overcall. With a similar hand, an overcall might be superior to a double. Furthermore, a third hand may offer a pass as the wiser alternative to the other actions.

#216. Your RHO opens the bidding with 1♣ and you hold:

♠QT
♥Q62
♦AKQT75
♣A2

You should overcall <u>1NT</u>! It is influenced by the bidding objective of playing in NT before a minor suit. A club lead ensures seven tricks if the diamonds behave. A major-suit lead could bring disaster. Regardless, this is a "hand for discussion" long after the result is known.

Comment Regarding Defensive Bids

An understanding of Overcalls, Take-Out-Doubles, and Balancing is essential to good bridge. Balancing is the most difficult defensive bid to learn, and **cannot** be executed properly without the disciplined use of Overcalls and Take-Out-Doubles. After an opening bid on your right, marginal defensive hands (overcalls and doubles) should be passed. This leads to "balancing." Conversely, knowing partner will "balance" allows a more comfortable pass of the *marginal* hand.

CHAPTER TWELVE

MORE DEFENSIVE BIDDING

PART TWO: THE TAKE-OUT, OR

INFORMATORY, DOUBLE

In PART ONE of defensive bidding, which is a treatise on the Overcall, it was established that only one of the defensive bidders is in the "overcall seat." That is, he is directly <u>behind</u> the opening bidder.

The Take-Out Double is another defensive action. It is most often used by the player in the overcall seat, but it can be used by the other defensive bidder as well. There are many types of "doubles" in bridge, and players are sometimes confused regarding which "double" is which. From this point on, the word "double" will be used without the description of "take-out" and will have no other meaning unless so stated.

The double has its own nuances just as the overcall has, and there is NO similarity between the two actions.

Therefore, all guidelines are different. There are four components to the double. Each will be thoroughly covered in concept with supporting examples. They are...

1. REQUIREMENTS FOR A TAKE-OUT DOUBLE

2. MEANING OF A TAKE-OUT DOUBLE

3. RECOGNITION OF A TAKE-OUT DOUBLE

4. RESPONSES TO A TAKE-OUT DOUBLE

When studied as a defensive bid, the Overcall concept embraced a thinking process which was built on "winners" and "losers." It minimized the use of point-count, especially when responding to the overcall. In the study of the take-out double, however, less importance is placed on winners and losers and <u>greater emphasis</u> is placed on point-count, high-card structure, and card placement.

1. Minimum Requirements for a Take-out Double

A. <u>THE VALUE OF AN OPENING BID</u>:

When using the standard point-count method as a gauge or guideline, 13 points are needed. However, if you use the playing-trick method, 4½ tricks, which include 2½ defensive tricks, are required. Some players insist that a doubling hand should always possess 2½ tricks which can be relied on for defensive purposes. *Others feel that two tricks are sufficient when evaluating a hand for either "opening-bid" or "doubling" purposes.*

It should be understood that as a player reaches higher levels of skill and proficiency, he will occasionally become more flexible in taking certain actions. It is NOT suggested, however, that the requirements for an opening bid or a double be lessened. Altering the value of a hand for some take-out doubles may be reasonable when you know certain key cards are on your "right" because of the opening bid. This is "**favorable card placement**."

B. <u>SUPPORT FOR THE UNBID SUITS</u>:

Technically, the word "support" indicates a holding of at least three cards in a suit. Four-card support is ideal and is expected most of the time, especially in the major(s). A double should be avoided with <u>only</u> three cards in the unbid suits. The most common distribution for doubling is 4-4-3-2. Of course, the two-card holding is in the opponent's suit that was doubled.

Occasionally, the expected high-card strength can be lessened provided the doubler has perfect "shape" for his double. In the language of bridge regarding doubles, "SHAPE" indicates a 4-4-4-1 distribution. This perfect distribution compensates for a shaded double since the prospect of finding a comfortable suit-fit is increased.

The double should jolt partner into thinking about your hand rather than his own. **He should "see" your hand as <u>an opening bid and imagine your shape to be much different from the shape common to an overcall.</u>** When considering whether to make a double, be aware of two things. First, a hand with *minimum* opening-bid values **without** support for the other suits is a disciplined PASS, not a take-out double. Second, it **is** possible to double despite the lack of support in a given suit. However, to permit this, <u>the doubler must be able to bid again!</u> **This means he must have greater strength than a minimum hand** so that he can "correct" partner's response (which might not be favorable) to a suit of his own. This idea of "correcting" will be discussed at length under "double with correction."

The following examples illustrate strength, shape and support.

#217.

Opener	You
1♦	?
	♠KJ92
	♥AQ82
	♦42
	♣K95

Double! You have great support for the unbid suits and a very solid opening bid.

#218.

Opener	You
1♥	?
	♠AQ75
	♥65
	♦AJ2
	♣KT85

Double! Perfect support for the other major and a very strong hand for a "minimum."

#219.

Opener	You
1♣	?
	♠KT74
	♥Q953
	♦AQ92
	♣2

Double! As an opening bid, this is just marginal and it has only two defensive tricks. However, the shape is perfect, which is a plus for a doubling hand.

#220.

Opener	You
1♠	?
	♠J84
	♥K6
	♦AJ84
	♣KQJ2

Pass! This solid opener has a worthles ♠ Jack and only two hearts. Don't ask partner to bid if it may be embarrass ing. Let the bidding go and maybe you can join in later.

2. The Meaning of a Take-out Double

A. THE DOUBLE MEANS "BID, PARTNER"

I want you to bid on MY cards and MY values. My hand is good enough to bid but I am unwilling or unable to choose a suit. I probably do <u>not</u> have a good five-card suit <u>but</u> have support for anything. Imagine that I have bid the other suits and you just have to show a preference. In other words, **you** choose the suit for me! Don't worry about bidding a suit that I don't have.

B. TRUST ME, PARTNER

The doubler deserves to be trusted. He has met the requirements for a double which should preclude getting his partner into trouble. The double also asks partner to accentuate the <u>major suits</u> when he responds. Bid a four-card major before a five-card minor. At times, it may be wise to bid a three-card major before a four-card minor if this action allows the partnership to remain at a lower level.

3. The Recognition of a Take-out Double

Since there are several types of doubles in bridge, it is essential to sort them out and determine which double is informatory or take-out. Which double is the one that says, "I want you to bid, partner?" To determine whether a double is for "take-out," ask yourself two questions:

1. Has my partner doubled **THAT** bid at his first opportunity to do so?
2. Have I bid yet?

If the answer to the first question is yes, and the answer to the second question is no, then a take-out double has been executed.

IN A NUTSHELL, A TAKE-OUT DOUBLE IS RECOGNIZED AS SUCH WHEN THE DOUBLE WAS MADE AT THE FIRST OPPORTUNITY TO DOUBLE *THAT* BID **AND** THE PARTNER OF THE DOUBLER HAS NOT YET BID! The partner of the doubler may have passed, but a "pass" is NOT considered a bid.

Following are four bidding sequences which illustrate this topic. The problems are in the left-hand column with the comments in the right-hand column. Cover the answers while working the problems.

#221.

West	North	East	South
Opener	Part.	Resp.	**YOU**
1♠	DBL	Pass	?

Is this a take-out double? If so, prove it with a clear explanation.

Your partner, North, doubled the opening bid at his first opportunity. You haven't made a bid before his action so his double **IS** for take-out. You must bid as he asked.

#222.

South	West	North	East
YOU	Opener	Part.	Resp.
Pass	1♦	DBL	Pass
?			

Is this a take-out double?

You dealt and passed, after which the next player opened the bidding. Partner doubled at his first opportunity to do so. You have <u>not</u> bid yet, so **YES**, the double is for take-out. You must bid as he asked.

#223.

North	East	South	West
Part.	Oppt.	**YOU**	Oppt.
1♦	1♠	Pass	Pass
DBL	Pass	?	

It's your turn to do something so I hope you know whether partner has made a double asking you to bid. Has he?

North opened the bidding and was overcalled. That is quite normal. You and the guy with the funny haircut pass and partner says, "Double"! Does he really want you to bid? **OF COURSE.** This is his first chance to double and you have not bid. He has his heart suit <u>with</u> both diamonds and clubs. **SO BID, ALREADY!**

#224.

West	North	East	South
Opener	Part.	Resp.	**YOU**
1♥	DBL	2♥	Pass
Pass	DBL	Pass	?

Well, you understand how to tell whether a take-out double has been executed. What is your answer? Do you bid or not?

You know partner's double was for take-out. The opponent's raise took you "off the hook" with your lousy hand. Partner repeated his "call of the wild." He has a very good hand with all suits well-covered. He doubled twice asking you to bid, **SO DON'T LET HIM DOWN!**

4. Responding to a Take-out Double

It is in the area of responses to the double that we become quite restrictive in the use of point-count requirements. There are seven different responses to a take-out double, and each is recognized by either definitive point-count or by the use of reason and logic. *Remember, you are expected to respond to a take-out-double unless relieved of the obligation by an opponent's bid.*

A. <u>THE SIMPLE RESPONSE</u>:

Bidding a new suit in the most economical manner in response to a double indicates a point-count of zero to eight (0–8). These values show that you are bidding at the request of partner and you promise nothing. Eight points is about the maximum for this *simple response*. Examples follow.

<u>#225.</u>

Opener	Part.	Resp.	YOU
1♦	<u>DBL</u>	Pass	?

♠9862
♥J75
♦J864
♣98

What do you bid, if anything? Your hand is pretty awful.

Partner made a take-out double, didn't he? You weren't relieved of the obligation to bid, so honor his request and bid <u>1♠</u>. A simple bid by you promises nothing although you may have a smattering of cards.

<u>#226.</u>

Opener	Part.	Resp.	YOU
1♥	<u>DBL</u>	Pass	?

♠92
♥J43
♦Q9764
♣Q72

What bid do you make? Why?

The correct bid is <u>2♦</u>. You have honored the double and may have to play for eight tricks with diamonds as trumps. Partner knows you may have only four trumps, but if this is so, you certainly have only two spades. Why should this be true?

#227.

Opener	Part.	Resp.	YOU
1♣	DBL	Pass	?

♠Q963
♥T4
♦654
♣AT92

It's your turn to bid after partner made a double. Notice the clubs you have and remember that partner promised the other suits.

Bid **1♠** like you're supposed to. The double screams for the major suits, and you have one. Hopefully, the clubs will come in handy during the play. Also, this is pretty good for a "bad" hand. If the opponents keep bidding and get too high, you may have good values for defense.

#228.

Opener	Part.	Resp.	YOU
1♣	DBL	2♣	?

♠9742
♥J85
♦T842
♣K6

What do you bid? If you did, why one suit rather than the other?

The responder bid 2♣, which relieves you of the responsibility of bidding. Your bid is **PASS**. When the auction gets back to partner, if he has more, he can double again, in which case you would bid spades. If you were foolish enough to bid, I hope you chose spades rather than diamonds.

B. THE JUMP RESPONSE:

Despite the fact that partner said, "I want you to bid on my cards," you may have a genuine eagerness to get into the auction. This is shown by making a response in which you **jump** a level in the bidding OR bid naturally at the three-level. Either a jump or bidding at the three-level shows 9–11 points. To be sure, there are some nine-point hands which are poor and others that are terrific. This is a judgment area, and only experience will guide you in determining whether the "nine" is good or bad. When looking at your "nine," imagine partner's hand and try to judge whether a good fit exists and whether any of the high cards are wasted. The Jump Response is *limited, not forcing, and invitational*.

#229.

Opener	Part.	Resp.	**YOU**
1♦	DBL	Pass	?

♠AT84
♥K5
♦942
♣QJ82

You should be getting pretty good at this business, so what bid do you make now?

Bid **2♠**! You have a terrific hand in support and rate to take many tricks. The jump shows that you are "eager" to bid, not just responding because you were asked to. The jump-response **may** get the partnership to game.

#230.

Opener	Part	Resp	**YOU**
1♥	DBL	Pass	?

♠J3
♥742
♦K63
♣AQ942

What is the correct bid?

The double asks you to bid with emphasis on the other major (spades). You cannot oblige him there, but since partner also promised "support" for the other suits, bid **3♣** to show your good values.

#231.

Opener	Part	Resp	YOU
1♣	DBL	3♣	?

♠AQ82
♥KJ
♦83
♣7543

The responder just got in your way and certainly interfered with you. What do you do?

An auction such as this is common-place when the opponent attempts to pre-empt the bidding. Bid 3♠! This is an illustration of bidding "at the three-level" without a jump. Since the beginning of your bridge study, awareness of the "three-level" has been emphasized.

#232.

Opener	Part	Resp	YOU
1♣	DBL	2♣	?

♠AJT
♥2
♦KQ763
♣T965

There is no question that the opponent made it tough. What should you do?

Bid 3♦! This bid, like the previous example, shows 9-11 points because you are at the three-level. Failure to bid spades indicates three or fewer in that suit. Imagine partner's size and shape for his double and you will "see" a well-fitting hand that will play well.

C. THE FREE BID:

After partner makes a take-out double, the next player (opponent on your right) will frequently bid a new suit or he may raise the opener. What his bid shows is relatively immaterial at this point. You may have some values and wish to indicate this to partner despite the opponent's bid which relieved you of the obligation of answering the double. You can!

Provided you do not jump, a suit bid at the one- or two-level shows 5–8 points. This bid is called a "free bid" (in this case, a free response). The term is used to describe any bid which is voluntarily made as opposed to a bid made because of a force.

This is another scenario in which "imagining" partner's hand allows a reasonable bidding action. Picturing partner's hand and then matching it to yours for "fit" and "losers" is a technique which all good players develop. In the auction of 1♦-DBL-1♠-YOU, the 1♠ bid has relieved you of the responsibility of honoring partner's double. Picture partner's hand. He promised spades, hearts, clubs and an opening bid. Predicated on "losers," you might want to bid freely as in the two examples which follow.

#233.

Opener	Part.	Resp.	YOU
1♦	DBL	1♠	?

♠Q9
♥K98632
♦5432
♣8

If you bid, it must be at the two-level and you have only a King and a Queen. What do you do and why?

Bid 2♥! Picture partner's hand as spades, hearts, and clubs. He is short in diamonds so you should have little trouble playing for only five "losers." The failure to jump shows fewer than 9–11 with a desire to get into the auction. This is the free-bid of 5–8 points.

#234.

Opener	Part	Resp	YOU
1♥	DBL	2♥	?

♠Q9853
♥9742
♦K6
♣52

This should be an easy one by now. You know partner is short in hearts so some of your heart "losers" can be trumped in his hand. Bid 2♠! You will make it and he will be aware of your values because you did not jump but made a "free" bid.

D. THE PRE-EMPTIVE RESPONSE:

Pre-emptive hands occur with frequency, and you may be dealt one as Opener, as Overcaller, or as the Responder to either. A pre-emptive bid is designed to block the opponents from an easy path to their destination while not incurring an unreasonable penalty for your effort. Imagining "winners" and "losers" allows this bid to be used advantageously. If you held ♠QJ75432 ♥4 ♦8742 ♣3, and you knew that partner had 13 points with four spades, you should be certain that the opponents could make a game. All effort must be put forth to make it difficult for them to find their best spot, which might even be a slam.

A pre-emptive response to a double is a double- or triple-jump in a suit. This bid should not be confused with a simple jump-response which shows a reasonably good 9-11 points.

#235.

Opener	Part.	Resp.	**YOU**
1♦	DBL	Pass	?

♠4
♥KJ96432
♦432
♣76

This is a typical pre-emptive hand. Partner made a take-out double and your right-hand opponent passed.

You must bid a large number of hearts. The safest bid is 3♥. Let partner do what he wishes. If you are not vulnerable and the opponents are, perhaps a 4♥ bid might be in order. The pass by Responder might show some cards. If not, Opener probably has more than a minimum. No matter! Your pre-emption is necessary. Partner will know what to do.

#236.

Opener	Part.	Resp.	YOU
1♥	DBL	RDBL	?

♠Q987642
♥9763
♦Q8
♣none

The opponents fit. You have an image of partner's hand. What now?

Bid 4♠ immediately. Make this bid without regard for vulnerability. If allowed to play there, you will probably make it because of the screwy distribution. If the opponents bid to the five-level, they may be in jeopardy. DO NOT BID AGAIN!

E. THE ONE NO-TRUMP BID:

The 1NT response to a take-out double is much the same as the 1NT response to an overcall. There are two schools of thought regarding this bid. One is sound and rather conservative while the other is loose and aggressive. Unless a player is of expert quality, the former approach is far better for the partnership. Therefore, the 1NT response indicates about 9–11 points with no-trump shape and a willingness to take responsibility for the suit which partner doubled. It would be ideal to promise the values of an Ace, King and Queen, but the ideal is not always practical, so judgment is important.

Good judgment allows the bid to be used with a nice eight points with proper stoppers. Regardless, the 1NT bid shows a reasonable hand. The same good judgment will guide you to bid 2NT when holding a terrific 11 or 12 points with double stoppers. The 2NT response should encourage partner to go to game if possible.

#237.

Opener	Part.	Resp.	**YOU**
1♠	DBL	Pass	?

♠AQT
♥94
♦K984
♣T982

Partner asked you to bid on his cards. You happen to have two four-card suits. What bid do you make?

Your bid <u>must</u> be 1NT. This is about the minimum one should hold to make this response. Your bid is sound and partner should "see" the values necessary for the bid. He also should "see" the stoppers which you promise in the opponent's suit. The heart deficiency is of no concern as the doubler promised hearts.

#238.

Opener	Part	Resp	**YOU**
1♦	DBL	1♥	?

♠J3
♥Q6
♦AJ94
♣K9432

Partner made a take-out double after which the other opponent bid hearts. You have a terrific hand with five clubs so you have no reason to be shy. What do you bid and why?

Please don't consider bidding clubs. The correct bid is 1NT, and you are very close to a 2NT bid. With any luck at all, the club suit may set up for extra winners. Bridge concept and logic dictate that emphasis should be placed on reaching no-trumps before the minors if possible. You have the diamonds well-stopped and partner has promised spades, hearts and clubs REGARDLESS of the 1♥ bid by the opponent. Bid your cards and don't worry.

It is an accepted fact that playing a hand at 1NT with a minimum opening bid opposite a minimum-type response is often very difficult. When a take-out double has been made, a response of 1NT should have adequate high-card strength, not just a smattering of points with a stopper. The doubler may have about 11 or 12 high-card points plus distribution for his values. The distributional value is worthless in no-trump. An average double has twelve high-card points. Successful play at 1NT requires about twenty-one high-card points for the partnership. That is why the responder should have about NINE for his bid.

F. THE CUE-BID RESPONSE:

The cue-bid response to a double usually implies strength (12 points or more) but may also be used when the bidder is not sure of the final contract. A few players use it as a game-force, but most use the cue-bid only as a ONE-ROUND FORCE. A subsequent bid by responder will almost always be made. The "cue" is a tremendous asset when used carefully as the following examples and explanations illustrate.

#239.

Opener	Part.	Resp.	YOU
1♣	DBL	Pass	?

♠AQJ4
♥K32
♦KQT4
♣64

#240.

Opener	Part.	Resp.	YOU
1♦	DBL	Pass	?

♠AQ84
♥103
♦KQ104
♣432

With hand #239, a cue-bid of 2♣ is mandatory. Playing in game is assured and the concern is which game to bid. The cue-bid will make the doubler bid again. If he bids 2♠, jump to 4♠. If he bids 2NT, bid 3NT. If he bids 2♥, cue-bid (3♣) again. This implies, "you haven't satisfied me; please tell me more." At this point, the doubler would rebid hearts if he had five OR he would bid no-trump with a club stopper. If he fails to satisfy you with either bid, you then have to determine the final contract. It certainly should be the four-opposite-three "fit" in hearts.

Bid the same hand again, but pretend that the opponent opened with 1♦ which partner doubled. Again you would cue, and if partner bid 2♠ you would bid game in that suit. If he bid 2♥ or 3♠, you would bid 3NT.

Responder's actions are **PREDETERMINED**. It makes things simple when the *concept of predetermination* is applied because that concept influences each aspect of bridge, reduces "over-thinking," and makes many decisions become "automatic." You are the captain of the hand and you are the one who knows that game must be bid.

With hand #240, you have a nice hand, but not enough to guarantee game. Cue-bid 2♦! If partner bids 2♠, raise to 3♠. If partner bids 2♥, bid 2NT. Both the 3♠ and 2NT bids are invitational as they are "one short of game." Invitational bids always ask partner to bid the game if he has at least a QUEEN more than the minimum that he promised. The cue-bid allows greater latitude in exploring for the most complete information available.

There are other hands which illustrate the valuable use of the cue-bid. A "relay" cue-bid is used to handle two-suited hands with emphasis on the majors. A hand may be worth game or just a part-score, but the cue can ensure getting to the "right" contract. Examples #241 and #242 follow.

#241.

Opener	Part	Resp	YOU
1♦	DBL	Pass	?

♠AJT42
♥KQT73
♦2
♣73

#242.

Opener	Part	Resp	YOU
1♦	DBL	2♦	?

♠K9742
♥QT863
♦4
♣Q4

Hand #241. After partner makes a take-out double, you must reach game in one of the major suits. Partner rates to have at least one four-card major, but even in the worst scenario, he has a three-card major. Cue-bid 2♦! If he fails to bid a major, repeat the cue-bid. He will bid a major the second time. The opponents may add pre-emption to the bidding, but that shouldn't deter you from making your bid.

The possibility exists that an opponent could bid again and relieve partner of answering your cue-bid. If this happens, repeat the cue. The following hypothetical auction could occur with hand #241.

Opener	Part.	Resp.	YOU
1♦	DBL	Pass	2♦
3♦	PASS	Pass	4♠

Opener's 3♦ rebid (showing "extras") permitted partner to pass indicating a minimum double. A "free" rebid would indicate added values. The 4♠ repeat cue will get the job done. Logic and reason are the elements that enable players to understand bids whose meanings are not obvious.

Hand #242 is less valuable than the previous one. The correct bid is the 3♦ cue. Again, why guess which suit to bid when you can get partner to do it? If he doubled with four cards in one major and three cards in the other, he will bid the longer one in response to your cue.

G. <u>THE PENALTY PASS</u>:

The least frequent action when responding to a take-out double is the conversion of the double to a PENALTY DOUBLE. The conversion is made by passing partner's take-out double. It is called a "penalty pass" and should not be confused with a pass after being relieved of the obligation to bid.

The requirement for converting at the one-level is the assurance that you can take four tricks on defense with at least THREE in the trump suit. Logic determines this arithmetic. An opening bid (in this case, partner's double) should produce $2\frac{1}{2}$ tricks in defensive play. Sitting <u>behind</u> the opener, at least three tricks are almost guaranteed. Since the "doubler" promises nothing in the trump suit, you must accept the responsibility of taking the other four tricks.

#243.

Opener	Part.	Resp.	YOU
1♦	<u>DBL</u>	Pass	?

♠A4
♥762
♦KQT82
♣983

Partner doubled 1♦. With his cards in the other suits, you certainly can make something in no-trump. What do you bid?

This is a classic and, although opportunities for a low-level penalty double don't occur often, take advantage of it when you can. Why try to play a hand that you can defend? You can't get to game unless partner has "extras," and the more he has, the more the opponents go down. PASS!

#244.

Opener	Part.	Resp.	**YOU**
1♥	DBL	Pass	?

♠J72
♥J86432
♦642
♣5

You have six cards in the opponent's trump suit. It won't be easy to take them away from you. What do you bid?

This is a sucker problem. You have a simple 1♠ bid. If you pass for penalties, you live in a dream world. Declarer will make the hand more often than not, perhaps with over-tricks.

Although you have six trumps, YOU HAVE <u>NO</u> TRICKS, and that's what this game is all about—taking tricks.

Since you first developed an interest in learning bridge, repeated reference has been made to LOGIC and REASON. The answers to almost everything in the game can be found by using logic and reason. In this postulation of take-out doubles, the entire text makes sense if you just reason it out. Other aspects of the game make sense in the same way.

Take-out Doubles with Correction

The requirements for a take-out double were presented very clearly at the beginning of this portion of the text. Few difficulties should be encountered in accepting and understanding the basic premises of the take-out double. However, after the basic premises have been established, it is then extended into an advanced and subtle concept referred to as "double with correction." At times, it may seem as if there are contradictions in philosophy.

THE basic premise is that when a double has been made which correctly reflects size (an opener) and shape (support for the other suits), the doubler cannot bid again voluntarily.

If invited, he *may* bid again and if forced, he *will* bid again. Neither action is voluntary. His "limited values" may have been shown with his double. In principle, one does NOT bid the same values twice unless he has a mouth problem or is trying to get rid of a partner. With this to influence our thinking, we can theorize about the "double" and "correction." A garden-variety double of an opening bid of one of a suit constitutes making a bid at least equal in strength to that of the opener. If one were to double, and at his next turn bid again voluntarily, the value of that hand is three points greater than originally promised for each bid that is taken or each level that is reached. A sequence follows which illustrates this.

Opener	**PARTNER**	Responder	You
1♣	DBL	Pass	1♥
Pass	2♥!	Pass	?

The question mark is where you make your decision based on your cards plus the interpretation of partner's bid. His double showed an opening bid with support. He voluntarily bid again at his next opportunity.

The raise increased the bidding by one level which showed an additional three points. Three-point spreads are referred to as brackets. When he doubled, the message was, "I have an opening bid with support."

After bidding again, the further message was, "Correct your thinking because I have more. To be precise, I have 16–18 points." You probably would bid again if you had a good eight points.

In the same auction, if the doubler had bid 3♥ at his second opportunity instead of 2♥, he would have showed 19-21 points. Again, each new bid sends a message to partner to "correct" his thinking. You might bid game with a solid five points and certainly would bid it with 6-8 points.

Study the following deals, which illustrate this concept. In all three examples, West is the dealer and both sides are vulnerable.

#245.

	North		West	North	East	South
	♠QJ64		Opp.	**Partner**	Opp.	**YOU**
	♥KQT7					
	♦8		1♦	**DBL***	Pass	1♥
	♣A953		Pass	**(PASS)****Pass		
West		East				
♠A98		♠KT72

*The double shows an opening bid with support for the other suits. North has precisely what he promised.

**The pass indicates that North has no more than he announced with his double. Once this message has been sent, possible subsequent action may take place with no misunderstanding.

West: ♠A98 ♥A86 ♦KQ743 ♣42

East: ♠KT72 ♥J4 ♦A5 ♣JT876

South: ♠53 ♥9532 ♦JT962 ♣KQ

#246.

	North		West	North	East	South
	♠KQJ6		Opp.	**Partner**	Opp.	**YOU**
	♥KQT7					
	♦8		1♦	**(DBL)***	Pass	1♥
	♣A953		Pass	**(2♥)***	Pass	Pass
West		East	Pass			
♠A98		♠T742				
♥A86		♥J4	* The double shows opening bid			
♦KQ743		♦A5	values and support as promised.			
♣42		♣JT876				
	South		** The 2♥ bid shows added val-			
	♠53		ues of three more points which			
	♥9532		indicate 16-18 points, a second			
	♦JT962		bracket hand.			
	♣KQ					

#247.

	North		West	North	East	South
	♠KQJ6		Opp.	**Partner**	Opp.	**YOU**
	♥AQT74					
	♦8		1♦	**DBL***	Pass	1♥
	♣AJ5		Pass	**3♥***	Pass	4♥
West		East	Pass	Pass	Pass	
♠A98		♠T7432				
♥K86		♥J	*You know this by now! The			
♦KQ743		♦A5	major response of 1♥ is natural.			
♣43		♣T8762	**A big "correction" showing a			
	South		third-bracket hand (19-21			
	♠5		points). South (that's **YOU**, pal)			
	♥9532		has an easy game bid in hearts.			
	♦JT962					
	♣KQ9					

The three preceding examples clearly illustrate the method by which good players are able to make accurate judgments in bidding. If each player bids his cards exactly as he should, there will be few problems. The fact that South bid game in the last hand shows how trusting he is of partner.

Delving still deeper into the concepts of the take-out double, another nuance which merits attention concerns being deficient in a suit. The double states that IF the count is minimum, then support for all suits is promised. This must be amended. Because responder to the double will bypass a minor and do cartwheels to bid a major, the double may be slightly deficient in a minor.

With this new tool called "double and correction," it is further suggested that a deficiency can be found in any suit. This concept is evident in the following imaginary soliloquy.

> *"Partner, I have doubled. You can rely on me for sup-*
> *port for the other suits and an opening bid. Under these*
> *conditions, I will not embarrass you by being deficient*
> *in any suit you choose. However, I have the right to*
> *double while being deficient in a suit. If this occurs, my*
> *hand will be good enough so that if you bid the "wrong"*
> *suit, I can run to my own, which will be long enough*
> *and good enough to offer a safe haven regardless of your*
> *holding. If this happens, you must immediately adjust*
> *your thinking about my hand."*

#248.

Imagine that this hand is dealt to you:

♠A972　♥AKJ983　♦J7　♣2

The hand counts to 16–18 points, which is second bracket. It also is worth 6½ playing tricks if played in hearts. If your right-hand opponent opened the bidding with either 1♣ or 1♦, you should double. It's obvious that you have a deficiency in the other minor.

If partner responds in spades, you will raise him to show the added values. If he responds in the "other" minor, you can correct to the heart suit, which shows both the added values plus the good, long suit. There is no response that he can make which will cause trouble.

The following deals are shown in their entirety to illustrate the double with correction and to allow a study of the complete hand. Notice that the high cards are almost equally divided yet the ability to produce tricks is much different in each hand.

#249.

	North			East	South	West	North
	♠75			1♣	DBL*	Pass	1♦
	♥64			1♥	1♠**	2♣	(End)
	♦QJ952				(or)		
	♣JT83						

West		East		1♣	DBL*	1NT	Pass
♠QT3		♠42		Pass	2♠**	(End)	
♥853		♥AQT7					
♦A876		♦43			(or)		
♣Q76		♣AK942					

	South			1♣	DBL*	Pass	1♦
	♠AKJ986			Pass	1♠**		
	♥KJ92						
	♦KT						
	♣5						

The DBL* is normal and the following spade** bid is the correction. With no cards in the dummy, South will fail to make his contract while E-W can make a part-score.

Three auctions are shown with East Dealer in the adjoining column.

#250.

	North				
	♠765				
	♥T3	East	South	West	North
	♦86543	1♣	DBL*	2♣	Pass
	♣JT8	Pass	DBL**	Pass	2♦

West		East	Pass	2♥!!	(End)
♠J93		♠Q42			
♥Q85		♥74	* A take-out double showing at
♦J97		♦KQT	least minimum values (13–15).
♣Q763		♣AK942	** The repeat of the double shows

at least second bracket (16–18).

	South
	♠AKT8
	♥AKJ962
	♦A2
	♣5

Partner responds and !! The "correction" comes. This third action shows the self-sufficient suit and third bracket of 19–21.

East deals:

#251.

	North				
	♠AJ97				
	♥AKJ2	West	North	East	South
	♦5	1♦	DBL*	2♦	Pass
	♣KQ95	Pass	DBL**	Pass	2♠

West		East	Pass	3♠!!	Pass	4♠
♠5		♠Q83			
♥T43		♥Q875	* Again, a take-out double.
♦AQT63		♦KJ94	** The repeat of the double.
♣AJT2		♣83	

	South
	♠KT642
	♥96
	♦872
	♣764

!! The raise of partner's response, which is the third action showing 19–21 points. Partner is able to "see" your hand and bids the game.

West deals:

In example #250, South bid his hand as expertly as possible and must be confident that partner understood the bidding and acted correctly. The information sent by South took place in "three" steps. When partner was relieved by West after the first double, he then responded dutifully to the second double. When this was corrected to hearts, North should "see" four spades, six or seven hearts and 19–21 points. Regardless, he must pass short of game.

In example #251, South was relieved of bidding by East's raise of opener's diamond bid. The double was repeated, and South responded 2♣ with his bad hand. North took another action in the form of a raise to 3♣. This promised four-card support and 19–21 points. It is here that South demonstrated that he learned his lessons well. By "seeing" partner's hand and figuring his distribution and the probable high-card placement, South bid game on the basis of projecting no more than three losers. In the play of the hand, South can take eleven tricks if he handles the cards well.

Hands #252 and #253, which follow, are presented as a re-enforcement of the concept and the application of the double with correction.

#252.   ♠AJ42   ♥9   ♦AKJT75   ♣97

This is a fine second-bracket hand which has great possibilities for play with a little support from partner. If your right-hand opponent opened the bidding with either 1♣ or 1♥, you would "double" for take-out. It is only reasonable that partner would respond "wrong," which is in your shortest suit. Since your hand is of greater strength than a minimum, you have the obligation to bid again and correct both his action and his thinking. The auctions that would apply are:

Open.	**YOU**	Resp.	**PART.**		Open.	**YOU**	Resp.	**PART.**
1♣	DBL	Pass	1♥		1♥	DBL	Pass	2♣
Pass	(2♦)				Pass	(2♦)		
or 2♣	(2♦)				or 2♥	(3♦)		

In both instances, and as expected, the response by PARTNER to the double was made in the "short" suit which necessitated the correction. He should know the doubling hand (YOU) has a self-sufficient diamond suit and four spades. This is one of the great advantages of playing good jump overcalls because without the four-card spade suit, YOU would have jumped in diamonds immediately. Hands that fit the auctions above are almost always two-suiters and frequently are six-four in distribution.

#253.   ♠AKJ2   ♥9   ♦97   ♣AKQT75

This is a terrific hand! It is a third bracket (19–21 points) and certainly needs little from partner to make a game. If your right-hand opponent opened the bidding either 1♦ or 1♥, you would "double" for take-out fully expecting partner to bid "wrong" again. The auction may become sophisticated, but with this fine hand, you can get your messages across. Going way back to the basic principles of bridge, bidding is geared to playing in the majors, no-trump, and the minors, in that order.

a.

Open.	**YOU**	Resp.	**PART.**
1♦	DBL	Pass	1♥
Pass	(3♣)		

b.

Open.	**YOU**	Resp.	**PART.**
1♦	DBL	2♦	PASS
Pass	(DBL)	Pass	2♥
Pass	3♣		

c.

Open.	**YOU**	Resp.	**PART.**
1♥	DBL	Pass	2♦
Pass	(2♥)	Pass	?

d.

Open.	**YOU**	Resp.	**PART.**
1♥	DBL	2♥	PASS
Pass	(DBL)	Pass	3♦
Pass	(4♣)	Pass	?

In (a), you doubled the opening bid of 1♦ and after the 1♥ bid by **PARTNER**, the 3♣ bid showed hand (#253).

In (b), **PARTNER** was relieved of bidding. You put the double on again, and he bid 2♥, which you "corrected" to 3♣. Three separate actions by you, the doubler, showed first 13–15, then 16–18, and finally 19–21 points. Your distribution should be known to **PARTNER**.

In (c), the sophisticated cue-bid of 2♥ was necessary because **YOU** needed room to show your hand <u>without</u> passing 3NT. Since **PARTNER'S** 2♦ bid has already denied his having four spades, he should attempt to bid no-trump if he has a stopper in the opponent's bid suit. If not, he will bid *something* and **YOU** will then bid your club suit.

In (d), **YOU** asked partner twice to bid spades and he couldn't do it, so the 4♣ bid was all that was left. With a little something, he might bid the minor suit game.

Double and Correction to No-Trump

When a 1NT overcall is made, it shows a limited hand, proper stoppers, and the value of a 1NT opener. A partnership may be using 16–18 high-card points, $15\frac{1}{2}$–$17\frac{1}{2}$, or even 15–17 (experts only) as their no-trump range. Occasionally, a hand is dealt that is greater in value than the agreed-upon range for the 1NT overcall. Assume that the opening no-trump range is a standard 16–18 points.

A double, followed by a no-trump bid, shows 19 or 20 high-card points. If the double were followed by a jump in no-trump, it would show even more. It is imperative that the player who doubles conveys accurate information so partner (the captain) can properly decide on the final contract. After a "correction," the responder to a double will have to alter his thinking. The examples which follow are straightforward but incomplete. Once all the information is in, YOU must make the ultimate decision.

#254.

```
              North
              ♠KT6
              ♥762
              ◆QJ865
              ♣85
West                    East
♠Q5432                  ♠987
♥T43                    ♥KQ5
◆732                    ◆A4
♣94                     ♣AJT63
              South
              ♠AJ
              ♥AJ98
              ◆KT9
              ♣KQ72
```

Partner's double showed an opening hand with support for both majors. He will have what is promised <u>unless</u> he intends to correct, which he does in this example. The 1NT call shows a hand better than a 1NT opener. This counts to 18 and only one card is less than a 7-spot. No criticism is warranted for upgrading this hand a bit.

At your turn, add your six points and the five-card suit to partner's "19" and **YOU** should bid game in no-trump.

East Deals:

East	South	West	**YOU** North
1♣	DBL	Pass	1◆
Pass	1NT	Pass	?

#255.

North
♠AQ98
♥K5
♦KJ6
♣AQ52

West
♠542
♥AJ8
♦AQ5
♣KJT8

East
♠KT73
♥Q9
♦T432
♣974

South
♠J5
♥T76432
♦987
♣63

West Deals:

After the opening bid of 1♣, the double is made with intent to correct. There is some flexibility to the direction in which the bidding can go. For instance, if South **(YOU)** made a response to the double in either hearts or diamonds, the correction will be in no-trump. However, if the response were in spades, the correction would be a double raise in spades.

In the auction shown, **YOU** would respond 1♥, and after the correction which limits your partner's hand, **YOU** should get out of no-trump and back to the heart suit.

		YOU	
West	North	East	South
1♣	DBL	Pass	1♥
Pass	1NT	Pass	?

#256.

```
            North
            ♠T5
            ♥J974
            ♦542
            ♣K532

West              East
♠Q762             ♠A82
♥T532             ♥AQ8
♦96               ♦QT873
♣976              ♣JT
            South
            ♠KJ94
            ♥K6
            ♦AKJ
            ♣AQ84
```

East Deals:

			YOU
East	South	West	North
1♦	DBL	Pass	1♥
Pass	2NT	Pass	?

South was dealt a 2NT opener and East opened the bidding in front of him. South's only responsibility is to convey the message about his hand to North **(YOU)** for final determination.

The double starts things off by showing an opening bid and "support." After **YOU** have responded 1♥, partner jumps to 2NT. This shows a hand of 21 or 22 points. One might ask, "why not bid game directly with that much strength?"

Guessing whether to bid a game as a unilateral decision can be destructive when attempting to build a better partnership. **YOU** should bid 3NT with North's cards. Without the ♣K, game cannot be made.

♦ ♠ ♥ ♣

The following hands are for practice purposes and allow the reader an opportunity to study the "double" and some responses. The partnership is East and West and in each example, the opening bid is 1♣. This is done to facilitate the focus on the problem.

#257.

	West		East
	♠AJ43		♠KT5
	♥K65		♥98432
	♦AJ65		♦KQ2
	♣72		♣96

South	West	North	East
1♣	DBL	Pass	2♥ (End)

Note: East adds a little extra for his five-card major suit and jumps to show 9–11 points. This limits his hand and West becomes Captain. With an absolute minimum, West adds the values together and passes. The auction ends there, but if West had extras, he would have bid.

#258.

	West		East
	♠AQ32		♠K95
	♥A765		♥98432
	♦A765		♦KQ5
	♣2		♣96

South	West	North	East
1♣	DBL	Pass	2♥
Pass	4♥	(End)	

Note: After East jumps to show his 9–11 points, West takes over as captain. This time, he adds his 16–18 hand to what partner promised and bids the game. The "Principle of Captaincy" dictates that the player who <u>first</u> describes his hand within limits releases captaincy to partner.

#259.

	West		East
	♠KJ76		♠95
	♥AJ62		♥QT5
	♦A832		♦K97
	♣6		♣KJ872

South	West	North	East
1♣	DBL	Pass	1NT(End)

Note: East responds to the take-out double with a 1NT bid. This shows the values of an Ace, King, and Queen or a hand of equal value and takes full responsibility for the Opener's suit. It would be hard to find fault with the bid. West passes as there is no better place to play the hand. His singleton is of no value, so his hand is worth no more than the 13 high-card points. If East had better club spots, he might have converted the double into penalties.

#260.

	West		East
	♠KJ76		♠95
	♥AJ62		♥K95
	♦A832		♦974
	♣6		♣KQJT4

South	West	North	East
1♣	DBL	Pass	Pass
Pass			

Note: This is the conversion of the take-out double to a penalty double by the partner of the doubler. He promises four tricks with at least three in the trump suit. There is no question that East's action is sound. If South tried to escape, he would have been doubled at any contract. The power and length in the trump suit gives East the right to make this conversion. However, imagine that East's hand is changed to something such as: ♠95 ♥K95 ♦974 ♣98764. The distribution is the same but the power of the trump suit has disappeared. East *must* honor the take-out double and respond in a three-card suit.

#261.

	West		East
	♠K876		♠JT3
	♥AJ82		♥K5
	♦A876		♦Q32
	♣2		♣AJ765

South	West	North	East
1♣	DBL	Pass	2NT (End)

Note: East's jump to 2NT is precise. He has more than a 1NT bid, less than a cue-bid, and not enough club substance to convert to penalties. After being dropped in this bid, he probably wished he had passed and tried his luck at defending 1♣ doubled. East doesn't promise stoppers in the other suits, although he has help throughout the hand. The jump is <u>non-forcing</u> and West passes as he counts to "only" 12 in high-card points.

#262.

	West		East
	♠K876		♠QT3
	♥AJ82		♥K53
	♦A876		♦Q32
	♣2		♣AQ94

South	West	North	East
1♣	DBL	Pass	3NT (End)

Note: The 3NT jump response shows a hand of 13-16 high-card points. It denies a four-card major suit and promises absolute protection against the suit which was doubled. It can be compared to a 2NT response to an opening bid. Any consideration of passing the double for penalties should be abandoned with only four pieces of trump. Five or six cards should be held in the trump suit for penalty purposes.

#263.

	West		East
	♠AJ54		♠2
	♥KJ8		♥AT9432
	♦AJ92		♦K54
	♣98		♣653

South	West	North	East
1♣	DBL	Pass	4♥ (End)

Note: East should bid the game because his hand is worth more than it counts. The six-card suit is dynamite and if partner had opened 1♥, East would have bid 4♥. If the count drives you crazy, then try to picture "losers." There are many combinations which, when opposite East, have <u>only</u> three losers. Remember, the double promised support plus opening-bid values.

#264.

	West		East
	♠AQ76		♠T32
	♥KJ54		♥983
	♦A98		♦T76
	♣76		♣Q832

South	West	North	East
1♣	DBL	Pass	1♦

Note: Whatever happens after the 1♦ bid is of no concern. Our attention is on East who has <u>no four-card suit</u> to bid. Don't panic! Don't pass! Don't bid 1NT without the proper values! What you must do is bid your cheapest suit, say a little prayer, and trust that somebody will take care of you. As your proficiency and knowledge expands, you will learn that there are subtle ways to escape a disaster with something like hand #264.

<u>#265.</u>

	West		East
	♠KQ94		♠875
	♥AJ62		♥3
	♦Q92		♦AKT765
	♣86		♣J95

South	West	North	East
1♣	DBL	Pass	2♦ (End)

Whether one counts length for the extra diamonds or shortness in the heart suit, the hand counts to 9–11 and, therefore, the jump is warranted. It is non-forcing and West will pass. The ♣ J should be discounted as should any J or Q in the opponent's suit UNLESS it is being valued for no-trump play.

<u>#266.</u>

	West		East
	♠AJ9		♠KQ32
	♥KQ84		♥A983
	♦KJ984		♦A6
	♣3		♣974

South	West	North	East
1♣	DBL	Pass	2♣
Pass	2♥	Pass	4♥ (End)

Note: East's cue-bid of 2♣ is the strongest possible response to a take-out double. It is forcing to either 2NT or a suit agreement. Although it is not guaranteed, most hands reach game after a cue-bid has been used. After a cue-bid has been answered, a **new suit** by the cue-bidder is FORCING. In the above example, if East had a little less, he would have raised the 2♥ bid to 3♥ and this is not forcing. It is *expected* that the cue-bidder will have 12 or more high-card points (an opening bid) and a hand not suited to a no-trump response. Frequently, he will have a 9-11 point hand with both majors. The intention of the cue-bidder is to get the doubler to bid one of the majors and then raise him to three. At times, the opponents don't co-operate and the cue bid may have to be used at a higher level. If North had raised the opener to 2♣, East would have had to bid 3♣. If North had bid 3♣, East would bid 4♣.

#267.

West	(a) East	(b) East	(c) East
♠KJ97	♠A862	♠AQ62	♠AT62
♥AQ53	♥92	♥J2	♥J2
♦A43	♦Q9862	♦K9862	♦Q9862
♣86	♣75	♣75	♣AK

South	West	North	East
1♣	DBL	Pass	?

Note: After South opened the bidding 1♣, your partner (West) doubled. North passed and with each of the three examples, what bid do you make? With (a), your bid should be 1♠. It is correct to forgo bidding a five-card minor for a four-card major. In (b), the correct bid is 2♠. In (c), the correct bid is a cue-bid, and if partner's answer is in hearts, you then "correct" to 3NT. If his answer is in spades, you raise to game. With the hand shown in which he has four cards in each major, he may choose to relay the cue back to you to convey this message. It is a little fancy to be sure, but very, very logical.

CHAPTER THIRTEEN

ACTIONS OVER THE TAKE-OUT DOUBLE

You probably are familiar with some of the next portion of text, but it will not be surprising if much of the material is absolutely new. The concept to be explored and developed is that which is called "actions *over* the double."

It may be necessary to read and re-read the text several times in order to grasp the full significance of this vital part of bidding and partnership understanding. The thrust of the concept is directed to only one player, that is, the Responder to the Opening Bidder after the opening bid has been doubled. There is a direct relationship between this action and the "Captaincy Principle."

The Captaincy Principle comes to bear in many areas of the bidding structure, and it is this principle which allows one of the partners to "get out of the way" so the other can make a reasonable, and hopefully a winning, decision.

A limited opening bid releases captaincy to Responder and, conversely, a limited response releases captaincy to Opener. An Overcaller, even though the parameters of his strength may be wide, essentially releases captaincy to his partner. A player who makes a take-out double, whether he acts again or not, releases captaincy to his partner.

Each player in a partnership that understands the concept of captaincy and believes in the accuracy of his partner's bidding can <u>usually</u> determine which of the two pairs at the table has the balance of strength and therefore which pair "owns" the hand.

Once ownership is determined, like "squatters' rights," it gives the partnership a certain claim that should never be surrendered or compromised. *The claim is that the partnership has the right to either play the hand or to defend if it seems to be more fortuitous.* It is often difficult for Opener to determine if he and partner own the hand or if it belongs to the opponents. Therefore, in order to make it easier for Opener to know, any action taken <u>over</u> a double should be tied into a point-count or a trick-taking posture that can be understood by Opener.

The method which is recommended here is specially designed to give the average player the tools with which to compete favorably against better players who have an edge. It incorporates that which is widely accepted as "standard" with slight variations in order to create a definitive partnership structure. The basis for having a definitive form is to combine the knowledge of what the partnership is doing with a concept that dictates that "if all things are about equal, whoever owns the spade suit probably owns the hand."

The actions are as listed and will be considered separately:

1. Redouble
2. Bid of a suit
3. Pass to defer action
4. Pass (no cards)
5. Bid one no-trump
6. No-trump jump

1. Redouble

This action is the pivotal action for Responder. Standard bidding dictates that the redouble shows 10 or more points and usually implies shortness in the Opener's suit. This is ambiguous because in the *Official Encyclopedia of Bridge* and every other authoritative writing, when an illustration is given of a hand with <u>only</u> 10 high-card points, it is always something like an Ace and two Kings. A hand such as that is very strong opposite an opening bid and when the distributional values are counted, it often adds to an opener. There are no examples given in which Queens and Jacks make up the redouble. Is the redouble supposed to show ten *high-card* points or ten points including distribution? Is the redouble supposed to indicate *primary* high-card points, or *any* high-card points? Is the redouble supposed to indicate whether we should be in game or in a part-score? Players at the expert level have no problem with any of this. However, almost none of the everyday players have the knowledge to handle these problems with success.

Therefore, **it cannot be correct to unilaterally state that with 10 points, one should redouble!** A slight variation in the evaluation of the redouble can make bidding easier and more clearly defined when a hand is in the 10-point "twilight" zone.

For instance, after partner opens the bidding with 1♦, there is no justification for saying "redouble" with either of the following examples despite the fact that they both have ten high-card points.

♠Q2	♠QJ2
♥Q64	♥Q32
♦QJ632	♦Q95
♣K95	♣QJ43

More than ninety percent of all bridge players believe the redouble is correct here. They have either been told by inferior players or have read in a book that a redouble indicates ten points. Furthermore, many teachers do not explain this correctly. Increase the point-count for a redouble to a minimum of a good 11 or 12 H.C.points and attach to it the message:

> *The redouble guarantees that we own this hand. Therefore, we should play in game most of the time, or at least at the three-level. If not, let the opponents play the hand doubled for penalties.*

#268. Partner, who is North, opens the bidding four different times with one of each suit, that is: 1♠, 1♥, 1♦, and 1♣, and the next player doubles. You are South with this hand:

♠72
♥AQ98
♦QJ86
♣KJ9

Your action **over** the double is shown and a full explanation follows.

(You)
North (partner)	East	South	West
1♠ or 1♥ or 1♦ or 1♣	DBL	RDBL	?

Opposite each opening bid, the redouble shows both the strength **AND** the commitment to game or penalties and it allows the opponents' bidding to take a natural course. For instance, West may pass.

In modern bridge, his pass shows no desire to bid, but in olden times, the pass leaned toward a penalty action which many players still adhere to and, if that sequence were to be passed around, partner would garner a "game score" for making 1♠ doubled and redoubled. However, West will often bid, which *has to benefit* you and your partner, the North-South pair. If East decides to bid, that is also beneficial because whatever action is taken by East or West, North-South has a "fielder's choice" of sorts. They can bid game in a major or no-trump or they can execute a penalty double.

The latter is unlikely unless East-West do something foolish. A very important point here is that when either North or South declares the hand, that player will have helpful knowledge concerning the location of most missing high cards and a very good idea regarding the probable distribution of the hand.

For instance, after a 1♥ opening bid, the redouble sets up a guaranteed heart game. If the opponents try to sacrifice, it is certain that the North-South pair will know what to do, including calling the paramedics.

After a 1♦ opening, the redouble again allows great flexibility in action and exploration of a final contract. No difficulty will exist in getting to 3NT provided North can take care of the spade suit and play it from his side of the table. 4♥ can be reached if it should be, and 5♦ is a possible game contract.

After a 1♣ opening, the North-South pair salivates in hopes that the opponents get frisky. But if the opponents don't step out of line, North-South will find a game. A subtle, but powerful, interpretation of the redouble allows the partnership to continue bidding without having to jump in order to create a "force" on partner. The force (at least to the "danger zone" of the three-level) is incorporated into the redouble action. The method is just beautiful, and Opener doesn't have to fear making normal bids because his partner may have redoubled with a bad 10.

The next two hands also exemplify South's redoubling action and illustrate continual bidding to get to the right spot. Example #269 is short in spades, as is #268 , and #270 poses no problem even though South is long in spades.

#269.
♠72
♥K4
♦KT953
♣AKJ8

#270.
♠Q752
♥KQ4
♦KT9
♣AT8

Again, you are South and partner opens the bidding with ONE in each suit. Hand #269 will be considered first.

	(You)		
North (partner)	East	South	West
1♠ or 1♥ or 1♦ or 1♣	DBL	RDBL	?

The opening bid is 1♠ and after your redouble, West will probably bid 2♥. If North has that suit, he may pass, double or rebid spades. If he passes or bids 2♠, your call is a natural 3♦ bid and the auction will continue with your partnership reaching game in spades, no-trump or possibly a minor. If the redouble had been made with less value, partner might pass 3♦ and a play for game might have been lost. In a nutshell, the little extra that is promised with the redouble is just enough to save important bidding room, which is necessary on many auctions.

After a 1♥ opening was doubled and you redoubled, West almost certainly bid 1♠. South (you) has no problem when the bidding comes back because of the natural bids available <u>including</u> a cue-bid if necessary. If West's 1♠ response is followed by Pass-Pass, 2♦ is forcing. If North rebids 2♥, South follows with 3♣ which should allow the partnership maximum information to assist in the final decision. If North now bids 3♦ in preference to 3♣, South can make his fancy cue-bid to try for 3NT.

With either a 1♦ or 1♣ opening bid, much the same thoughtful and reasonable bidding will take place in an effort to reach 3NT. Failing that, game in a minor is almost certain to be reached.

In example #270, no matter what North opens, if he is doubled, you, as South, must redouble. The hand is too powerful to consider any other action. You know that game will be played in a major or no-trump. The best that can happen is that West will respond to the double. By doing so, he will give some clue to distribution which will assist you or partner in the play of the hand.

2. Bid of a Suit

As noted in the *Official Encyclopedia of Bridge*, some players treat a new suit response over a double as forcing. A small minority bid exactly as they would have without the double. The recommended method is the one used by the majority of players. That is, a new suit response over the double is <u>weak</u>, NON-FORCING, and non-constructive! It should promise a five-card suit at the one-level and at least a six-carder at the two-level.

Depending on the vulnerability and the opponents' willingness to enter the foray, the Opener should have no trouble in assessing "ownership" of the hand. It probably belongs to the enemy, and it is usually best to exercise caution with minimum hands. The opponents know how to inflict penalty doubles, too.

There is no problem when raising the Opener's suit as all raises are weak and offer no more than a play for the contract (provided partner has no more than a minimum opener) at the level at which the response is made. The following hands are held by South. No matter what North's opening bid is, South should have no difficulty in taking a reasonable action with each example hand.

#271.	#272.	#273.	#274.
♠QJ9765	♠4	♠942	♠9743
♥42	♥QT8742	♥Q86	♥A862
♦2	♦J9853	♦K743	♦QJ5
♣Q852	♣4	♣J85	♣42

<u>WITH #271,</u> your call is in bold type with an accompanying explanation in response to each suit opener.

		(You)	Repeat #271
North	East	South	
1♠	DBL	**4♠**	♠QJ9765
1♥	DBL	**2♠**	♥42
1♦	DBL	**2♠**	♦2
1♣	DBL	**2♠**	♣Q852

After 1♠, this 4♠ bid is highly pre-emptive and should cause some difficulty for the opponents even if they have greater strength. Your contract may make, but you will get no worse than a small minus if EW make a penalty double.

After either 1♥ or 1♦, the 2♠ bid is about the best you can do to disrupt the enemy and show a bad hand with long spades.

After 1♣, the 2♠ bid is correct but, if partner forces, you will show club help. Also, if the opponents' bidding is powerful, you may show the club assistance to suggest a "sacrifice."

WITH #272,

		(You)	Repeat #272
North	East	South	
1♠	DBL	2♥ or 3♥	♠4
1♥	DBL	4♥	♥QT8742
1♦	DBL	3♥ or 4♥	♦J9853
1♣	DBL	3♥	♣4

After 1♠, bid 2♥ if vulnerable, 3♥ if not. Pre-emption is very important provided you stay within a reasonable level to make sure any defeat is not catastrophic.

After 1♥, the jump to game is mandated, and a sacrifice is possible if the opponents bid 4♠. After 1♦, a jump to 3♥ or 4♥ can be followed by 5♦ if necessary, again as a sacrifice. After 1♣, a 3♥ bid is the limit.

WITH #273,

		(You)	Repeat #273
North	East	South	
1♠	DBL	2♠	♠942
1♥	DBL	2♥	♥Q86
1♦	DBL	2♦	♦K743
1♣	DBL	1♦ or 2♣	♣J85

In each instance, the best you can do is show a bad hand and run for the woods as fast as you can.

WITH #274,

		(You) South	Repeat #274
North	East		
1♠	DBL	3♠	♠9743
1♥	DBL	3♥	♥A862
1♦	DBL	2♦	♦QJ5
1♣	DBL	Pass	♣42

After 1♠, the 3♠ bid is about right. Partner stands a good chance to be successful. You should be reluctant to defend against 3♥, but if you like the hand for defensive purposes more than I do, bid only 2♠ and defend when and if the enemy bids 3♥. After 1♥, make your bid of 3♥ now rather than waiting to compete against the opponent's spade bid. Prod them to the level at which you are willing to sell out without placing your side in jeopardy.

After 1♦, even a bid of 2♦ might be risky. Take it easy, as the hand is probably theirs. After 1♣, the same as after 1♦. DUCK!

3. Pass and Defer Action

The act of *"deferring action"* is used sparingly by most players because they don't understand "action over the double." It is *the* most important element of the concept. By strengthening the redouble, ownership of a hand is clear-cut and decisions are easy. But how about the hands which are less than a redouble but are much better than a "poor" hand?

When the Responder to an opening bid has a minimum

count of a solid seven points (in the form of a trick-and-a-half) and is in the range UP TO the redouble, whether to play or defend a given hand has to be determined. The suits which are being bid by either side and the level at which a **point of no return** has been reached will indicate which action to take.

Under these circumstances, it is frequently best to defer making a decision in order to gather additional information which will assist in determining the best action. Incorporating both the ownership of the spade suit and the danger of the three-level as the keys to a contested auction, the following hand and explanation will illustrate the concept. You are South and hold:

♠A43
♥AT94
♦42
♣JT86

Your partner, North, opens the bidding with 1♠, which is then doubled by East. It doesn't take a genius to determine that North-South can make a few spades. HOWEVER, IT IS FAR BETTER TO PASS (defer action) for now. Allow West freedom to bid. This gives partner information about distribution and possible card placement which will be valuable to him when declaring at spades.

Also, **YOU** might choose to double for penalties and defend against either 2♥ or 3♣. The opportunity to make a choice comes from deferring action. The layout is here. Study it and read the continuing text from a theoretical point of view.

#275.

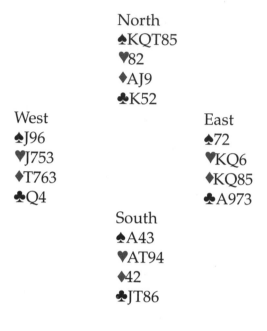

North
♠KQT85
♥82
♦AJ9
♣K52

West
♠J96
♥J753
♦T763
♣Q4

East
♠72
♥KQ6
♦KQ85
♣A973

South
♠A43
♥AT94
♦42
♣JT86

The Bidding:

North	East	South	West
1♠	DBL	**PASS**	2♥
Pass	Pass	**DOUBLE!**	?

The bidding can't be criticized, but the takeout double would have been better if East had a fourth heart. West's expected heart response points out the danger of not having full support for the other major. If South failed to defer action and chose a 2♠ raise, that would have been the final contract.

What a shame! The pass didn't preclude a spade raise later. For instance, if West had a five- or six-card diamond suit with only three hearts, he would have called 2♦. No problem for South as he then would have bid 2♠. With the cards as they are, North is waiting to take care of the rascals with a double if they try to escape to 3♦ after being doubled at 2♥.

If West bid 2♦ rather than 2♥ originally. It would be passed to South, who would then bid 2♠. The fact that South first passed and then bid conveys to North that partner has at least a trick-and-a-half and was "deferring action." The 2♠ bid will either be passed out OR if either opponent tries 3♦, North will double because of his knowledge of the combined hands. Just beautiful.

The effectiveness of this method is that one partner assists the other in cooperatively determining ownership of the hand for either bidding or doubling purposes.

4. Pass with No Cards

This, of course, is the easiest action to take when partner's opening bid has been doubled. You can see your cards and are aware that little, if any, strength exists. Partner should be aware that your pass may be "deferring action" but in no way should it influence what he does. It is presumed that he will bid or act on his values and not on "expectations" from you. The three examples which follow illustrate the obvious. The auction is complete with your hand shown.

#276.

Part.	Opp.	**YOU**	Opp.
1♣	DBL	**Pass**	1♠
P	P	**Pass**	

♠76
♥8532
♦8532
♣Q74

#277.

Part.	Opp.	**YOU**	Opp.
1♥	DBL	**Pass**	1♠
2♥	2♠	**Pass**	P
P			

♠8532
♥853
♦765
♣Q74

#<u>278</u>.

Part.	Opp.	**YOU**	Opp.
1♠	DBL	**Pass**	2♥
P	P	**Pass**	

♠9762
♥42
♦763
♣7654

There is an outstanding similarity in each example with your hand being consistently poor. More important, there are subtleties about which you should be aware. In #276, with the bidding ending so quickly, either an opponent made an error or your partner (the Opener) has spades and has nothing more to say.

#277 is more interesting because after the double was responded to, your partner, knowing you may have "nothing," bid again freely, which indicates that he has better than a minimum hand. The opponent who doubled <u>also</u> bid again, indicating that he has additional values. Guess what! There is little left for you and the guy in the other chair, so even though you have support in partner's suit, some of partner's values are in front of the doubler and the wisest action you can take is to run for the woods.

Making a bid on #278 is tempting but, without a trick, there is no way to justify a competitive bid of 2♠. The roof may cave in and/or the opponents may be given a second chance to improve themselves. Go quietly!

5. The One No-Trump Bid

This action over the double is misunderstood by too many players and is very often misused. The 1NT bid directly over the double shows a hand which is mildly constructive in size and fully descriptive in shape. It indicates a hand which is best shown in one thrust.

At the same time, it assists partner, the captain, in calculating the hand for defensive purposes. The strength of the 1NT bid is about nine points in high cards. In some instances, it may be only eight or may be even 10 or 11. It may be helpful to envision the point-count values as that of an Ace, a King, and a Queen or three Kings, give or take a little. When the Responder bids 1NT directly over the double, he relieves his left-hand opponent of the obligation of bidding, thereby waiving the opportunity to catch that opponent in a penalty double situation. Since the 1NT bid is voluntary, it must be concluded that it was made because no favorable defensive posture was present. The 1NT bid may be partially pre-emptive. If the opponent should bid "freely," penalty actions may follow.

The two examples which follow show the complete deal. West opens the bidding and East acts over the double.

#279.

	North	
	♠J64	
	♥AQT2	
	♦K986	
	♣K2	
West		East
♠Q5		♠KT72
♥9743		♥KJ5
♦A4		♦QJ75
♣AQ853		♣94
	South	
	♠A983	
	♥86	
	♦T32	
	♣JT76	

#280.

	North	
	♠AQ75	
	♥42	
	♦AJ84	
	♣J76	
West		East
♠J43		♠KT62
♥AQT73		♥K5
♦T2		♦Q976
♣AT5		♣Q83
	South	
	♠98	
	♥J986	
	♦K53	
	♣K942	

West	North	East	South		West	North	East	South
1♣	DBL	1NT	2♠(?)		1♥	DBL	1NT	2♣(?)
Pass	Pass	**DBL**			Pass	Pass	**???**	

Hands similar to these occur constantly. It is a shame that the majority of players fail to handle garden variety problems in an effective and profitable manner.

In #279, after partner's 1♣ opening bid was doubled, East bid 1NT. The reasoning is sound. If he had passed to defer action or redoubled (with 10 points), he still would have bid 1NT after South bid any suit at the one-level. Bidding 1NT immediately gained a little pre-emption against South, alerted partner to the presence of some high cards, and showed good distribution for no-trump play. South, meanwhile, is in a terrible bind with four spades and just enough to make a free-bid. Should he bid or should he pass? If he bids 2♠, East will double for penalties.

In #280, much the same reasoning occurs. After the double, East has no desire to defend against 1♠ IF that is South's bid. His 1NT bid is descriptive and sure enough, South bids at the two-level. At his turn, East should double for penalties. Ownership of the hand is a good enough reason for the penalty double. Occasionally, the opponents will make their doubled contract (not this time) but in the long pull, they are destined for disaster.

6. The Two No-Trump Jump:

There is no natural meaning for this bid because every strength-showing and/or weak-showing bid has been illustrated and described by well-defined actions. With any hand of good no-trump shape and opening values, a redouble would have been used. Therefore, some players have adopted a method from the system called ACOL in which the jump to 2NT over the double shows a hand that is invitational (but not forcing) to game in partner's suit, lacking in great defensive posture, and relatively long in trumps. This trump length tends to negate partner's defensive strength in his suit and alerts him to be offensive-minded. The method described is called the JORDAN CONVENTION.

The bidding and cards shown as example #281 highlight the use of the convention by West and East. The entire hand is then shown for your study and examination.

#281.

West	East		West	North	East	South
♠K7	♠43		1♥	DBL	**2NT***	?
♥AK975	♥Q843					
♦9643	♦AK85					
♣K2	♣765					

The auction is not completed but the depleted defensive strength is illustrated. East's heart length, when added to partner's heart length for an opening bid, diminishes the potential defensive values in that suit. There is also a very good chance that the Opener may have a spade honor and if so, it is probably trapped. The *Jordan 2NT response causes the opponents some difficulty. The entire deal follows:

The entire hand:

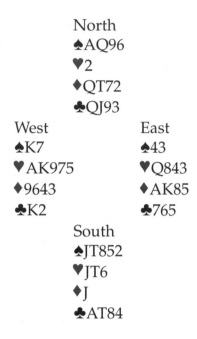

```
                        North
                        ♠AQ96
                        ♥2
                        ♦QT72
                        ♣QJ93
            West                    East
            ♠K7                     ♠43
            ♥AK975                  ♥Q843
            ♦9643                   ♦AK85
            ♣K2                     ♣765
                        South
                        ♠JT852
                        ♥JT6
                        ♦J
                        ♣AT84
```

The Bidding: West   North East   South
               1♥   Dbl   **2NT**   ?

North–South can make a spade game with ease. West should NOT consider any penalty double; that would be a disaster. The best East-West can hope for is that the opponents fail to bid their game. South, if he understands the bidding, will <u>NOT</u> pass! The use of this conventional bid occurs infrequently and conventions which are rarely used are too often misused.

♦ ♠ ♥ ♣

CHAPTER FOURTEEN

EVEN MORE DEFENSIVE BIDDING

PART THREE: BALANCING, OR, RE-OPENING THE BIDDING

The Overcall and the Take-Out-Double are defensive bids which occur very often. Another defensive bid, Balancing, is used less frequently. It is the most difficult of the defensive actions to master, a very important one to know, and the one in which the greatest number of errors is made. Balancing incorporates much of the philosophy of the overcall and the take-out double, especially the responses to it. The biggest difference, however, is that when balancing, the acts of bidding or doubling are often executed with hands of less strength than normally expected from a bidder in the overcall seat. Balancing, which is almost an art-form, **must** be mastered if you desire to play bridge well.

Question: What is meant by *BALANCING?*

Balancing is a bidding action which is taken when the opponents have bid and stopped at a low-level. Their failure to continue bidding indicates that the other partnership (which has not bid) might have enough strength and the proper shape to contest the auction. The decision to bid under these circumstances is tantamount to waiting until "the coast is clear."

Question: Which player executes the act of *BALANCING?*

Either partner may be in a position to balance. When two passes follow an auction, the player in the last "position," who may "pass" and end the auction, is the one who may balance. This position is referred to as the "balancing seat," the "dead seat," or the "pass-out seat." He could be in either the second seat or the fourth seat after an opening bid. Examples:

West	North	East	South		West	North	East	South
1♥	Pass	Pass	**Balance**		1♦	Pass	1NT	Pass
			Position		Pass	**Balance**		
						Position		

In the first example, South is in fourth seat. If he passes the auction is over. He may "protect" North's pass in this position. In the second example, where a full round of bidding has taken place, North (second seat) is now in the position that will end the auction if he passes.

Question: Why do so few players understand and execute *BALANCING?*

The three reasons which are most often given for a player's failure to learn how to balance are (1) the irresistible and natural tendency to bid prematurely when holding points even when a correct bid doesn't exist, (2) the modern tendency to get "in and out" of the bidding with very light hands and (3) a total mistrust of partner's ability to "protect" a hand which has passed. In England, the act of balancing is quite accurately called PROTECTION.

Question: Why is *BALANCING* such a very important action?

It is very important because (1) partnership confidence and reliability is strengthened which in turn (2) lessens the number of poor overcalls and shaky take-out-doubles. After an opening bid, too many players overcall and/or double without proper values <u>because of the fear that they may be "shut-out" of the bidding.</u> Knowledge that the partnership can and will balance when necessary lessens this fear and allows greater comfort when passing with marginal hands.

Question: Why is *BALANCING* rarely discussed and almost never taught as part of the average bridge teacher's curriculum?

The concept of balancing is subtle and most players, teachers included, do NOT understand it. Balancing is the outgrowth of "passing" after the opponents open the bidding. Few players possess the discipline and the knowledge of how and when to pass which in turn means players do not get experience and practice in balancing.

Balancing is frequently an outgrowth of a TRAP PASS! In Bridge jargon, the entire scope of balancing is usually thought of in the context of Traps and Balances. Therefore, it is necessary to understand what is meant by a "trap pass."

Your hand is ♠K6 ♥AQ98 ♦A643 ♣42. This is a nice opening bid but the man on your right is the dealer and he opened the bidding with 1♥, the suit you would have opened if he had passed. You have been "trapped" out of the bidding. You have no suit with which to overcall and if you double, it is for take-out and partner will bid. If you call 2♥, it is a cue-bid showing a hand much different from what you hold. I repeat, you have been trapped, so you have no alternative other than a **PASS**. This is a *TRAP PASS*.

Other examples are less dramatic but very consistent with the idea of being trapped. In almost all instances, the true trap will reflect a holding of at least four cards (but sometimes three) in the opponent's bid suit. It will have values with which to bid but no action which will accurately describe the hand. Following are three illustrations. East deals and opens the bidding and the next seat (the overcall position) is South.

(a)		(b)		(c)	
East	South	East	South	East	South
1♥	?	1♠	?	1♣	

(a)	(b)	(c)
♠62	♠K982	♠4
♥J9642	♥A653	♥K532
♦AKQ	♦KT73	♦AKJ8
♣K72	♣A	♣AQ97

Note that South holds cards in the opponent's bid suit in each of the hands. A true trap! In addition to this phenomenon of holding cards in the opponent's suit, one will often hold other hands which are good in value but poor in shape. It is best to pass under this circumstance, also. This pass is a type of trap. An imperfect bidding action on hands such as these would be terribly misleading to partner.

Question: What simple clues might assist a player in knowing when to BALANCE?

There are three factors which indicate when a balancing action <u>might</u> be taken. First, use your "ears" and listen to the bidding carefully. When the opponents quit bidding at the one or two-level, they invariably hold "minimum" hands. This means that you and your partner *probably* (1) have strength, and (2) may have a good "place to play."

Second, you should tend to be "short" in the opponent's bid suit. Balancing when holding the opponent's suit is usually bad judgment. Let him experience the difficulty of playing in a suit contract when the trumps break poorly.

Nevertheless, there are occasions when it is clear-cut to balance despite holding cards in the opponent's suit. Third, you should always have good major-suit holdings when balancing against the minors or no-trump, and guaranteed spade support when balancing against clubs, diamonds or hearts.

♦ ♠ ♥ ♣ **VERY IMPORTANT** ♠ ♥ ♣ ♦

Question: What values should be held in the hand that executes the *BALANCE?*

Balancing with a "suit-bid" at either the one- or the two-level promises a minimum of <u>5</u> or <u>6</u> high-card points. This is less than what is normally expected for a simple over-call. Balancing with a "double" at the one- or two-level promises a *minimum* of <u>9</u> or <u>10</u> high-card points, which is a King or an Ace less than what is expected for a normal take-out-double. Of course, vulnerability must be considered as well as the place (suit or no-trump) in which the final contract might play.

A Balancing <u>Bid</u> After an Opening Suit-Bid Has Been Passed

<u>#282</u>.

West	North	East	South
1♣	Pass	Pass	?

You are South and hold each of the following hands.

(a)	(b)	(c)
♠AQ92	♠3	♠8432
♥3	♥AQ92	♥AQ
♦9832	♦9832	♦Q9643
♣QJ92	♣QJ92	♣J9

Knowing *when to balance* depends on the ability to make an **ASSUMPTION** and do simple arithmetic. Consider the above auction.

The 1♣ bid by West is passed by his partner (East) who would have bid with six (maybe five) points. If you **ASSUME** that East has about <u>three</u> high-card points and **ASSUME** that the Opener (West) has about <u>thirteen</u> high-card points, their strength added to what you hold is about <u>twenty-five</u> high-card points.

Where are the remaining high-card points? Some, if not all, are in *your* partner's hand. Why didn't partner bid? There are three possible reasons. (1) He has the opponent's opening bid-suit. (2) He has cards but an *inability* to bid. (3) He has less strength than anticipated and the opening bidder has more. Yet, if the opening bidder has <u>sixteen</u> high-card points, doesn't that leave <u>twelve</u> for your partner? So...

With (a) bid 1♠!   With (b) Pass!   With (c) bid 1♦!

A simple one-level suit-bid in the balancing seat shows from **five to ten** high-card points. It <u>may</u> be only four-cards long and may not be very good. When a suit-bid is made in the balancing seat at the two-level, or when vulnerable, it shows from **five to as many as thirteen** high-card points. A five-card suit is expected but its strength may be less than required if the bid were made in the overall seat.

Conclusion: *You may "borrow" values from partner when balancing in a suit-bid.*

The hands above are identical in strength, but in (b), the Pass is correct. The reasoning is subtle. South **ASSUMES** that the opponents have a spade fit which may be found if the auction is re-opened. In the long run, the pay-off for defending against the 1♣ bid is substantial. The ownership of the spade suit is fully discussed in the next paragraph.

The Power of the <u>Spade Suit</u>

When considering certain bidding problems, special consideration is given to the ownership of the spade suit. If the strength of a hand is divided relatively equally between two partnerships, the pair that possesses the spade suit invariably has the right to play the hand or dictate how high the opponents must bid in order to compete. Owning this "master suit" allows that pair a unique position in auctions where both sides are bidding. When both sides have strength with which to bid, the pair without the spade suit frequently puts themselves in jeopardy if they have to bid higher to compete against the pair with the spade suit. This concept bears repeating so remember it well! **All things being equal, the pair with the spade suit usually owns the hand, so stay alert when both sides are bidding.**

A Balancing Double After an Opening Suit-bid Has Been Passed

As South, what call do you make with each of the following hands?

#283.

West	North	East	South
1♣	Pass	Pass	??

♠K986
♥QT85
♦AJ6
♣J2

#284.

West	North	East	South
1♦	Pass	Pass	??

♠K986
♥QT85
♦AJ6
♣J2

#285.

West	North	East	South
1♥	Pass	Pass	??

♠2
♥QT85
♦KJ86
♣AJ42

#286.

West	North	East	South
1♠	Pass	Pass	??

♠6
♥QT85
♦KJ86
♣AJ42

With #283, **DOUBLE**! This hand has *shortness* in the opponent's suit and great support for the other three suits with perfect support for the majors. Partner probably has some length in clubs and your side can score a "plus."

With #284, **DOUBLE**! This is less than perfect support, but partner will bend over backwards to bid a major. If he bids clubs, live with it as he probably has five of them. You can always apologize later (my glasses need cleaning) if disaster strikes.

With #285, **PASS!** Partner is probably short in the opponents suit, yet couldn't act. If you double, he will bid spades and that is unthinkable on your part. Being good at balancing means knowing when NOT TO ACT as well as when TO ACT.

With #268, **DOUBLE!** This is absolutely perfect. It is almost guaranteed that you and partner have a "fit" and that his failure to act is because he has some spades.

In each example, the recommended action would be the same if the hand were greater in strength. It is imperative that you be aware that the doubling action may be made with less strength than what is required in the immediate seat after the opening bidder.

A Balancing Jump Bid After an Opening Suit-Bid Has Been Passed

#287.			
West	North	East	South
1♥	Pass	Pass	??

♠KJ9732
♥AJ9
♦AJ
♣42

#288.			
West	North	East	South
1♦	Pass	Pass	??

♠6
♥AJ8532
♦42
♣AQ82

With #287, bid 2♠. This shows the values for a double but distribution which precludes doubling. In this case, nobody wants to hear partner bid diamonds or clubs.

With #288, bid 2♥. Again, the jump bid shows the strength of a double and certainly indicates a disdain for spades. If the opening bid on #288 had been 1♣, the same action (bidding 2♥) would be correct.

Whether a balancing action is a simple bid, a double or a jump bid, it is absolutely imperative that partner accurately assign a point-count "size" and a probable "shape" to the hand which took the action.

Balancing No-Trump After an Opening Suit-Bid Has Been Passed

When protecting partner, an allowance in value is given to whatever action is taken in the balancing position. The justification for acting is that the player who balances is really "borrowing" a few points from partner's hand in order to act at all. It is that fact which allows the balance to be made with less than would be expected if the same action had taken place in the immediate seat. In the immediate seat, a 1NT overcall normally shows a hand consistent in high-card points with the range used for an opening one no-trump bid. Knowledgeable players agree that the point-count range for a balancing one no-trump bid should be from 11 to 15 or 16 high-card points.

#289.				#290.			
West	North	East	South	West	North	East	South
1♥	Pass	Pass	??	1♣	Pass	Pass	??

♠Q2	♠KJ9
♥KJ82	♥8752
♦K83	♦Q74
♣AJ96	♣AKJ

With #289, bid **1NT**. This is a classic and absolutely descriptive bid. Partner is marked with enough cards for the contract to make. He may even have enough for a game. If he has eleven or twelve points, a high-percentage game is possible with most, if not all, of the remaining high cards being well-placed for declarer's play.

With the same hand, if the opening bid were 1♠, a balancing **double** would be made.

With #291, bid **1NT**. Even if partner held four hearts, this hand is suited for no-trump play. The same balancing bid would be tried against either a 1♦ or a 1♠ opening bid, although with some apprehension. However, if the opening bid were 1♥ only a **PASS** is acceptable.

Protecting partner is very difficult when you have a choice of bids in the balancing seat. You might be "on the edge" where a double, a jump bid or a no-trump call are considered. At times the wrong choice will be made—no question about it. When balancing, it is often best to imagine reasonable sizes and shapes of partner's hand and fit the images to the concept of winners and losers. Four examples follow. West opens the bidding 1♥ which is passed around to South in the dead seat. Any action could be right or wrong depending on <u>West's</u> hand.

Balancing with the Bid of 1NT

#291.

	North	
	♠AQ85	
	♥J973	
	♦52	
	♣J62	
West		East
♠J3		♠KT64
♥AQT82		♥54
♦J9		♦T86
♣AKT8		♣7543
	South	
	♠972	
	♥K6	
	♦AKQ743	
	♣Q9	

West Deals:

W	N	E	S
1♥	P	P	?

West's 1♥ bid goes to South who has too much to bid 2♦ and may be too high if he bids 3♦. His balance of 1NT is the *best choice*. If diamonds break, he will make at least eight tricks. If not, he will have trouble. If West continues with 2♣, South will compete with 2♦. The balancing bid has no guarantees for success but the **assumption** about partner's hand is usually on target. This hand is a typical example of how the strength is divided on similar auctions.

William J. August

#292.

North
♠AQ85
♥96
♦QT52
♣J62

West
♠J3
♥AQT82
♦J9
♣AKT8

East
♠T964
♥54
♦K64
♣7543

South
♠K72
♥KJ73
♦A873
♣Q9

West Deals:

W	N	E	S
1♥	P	P	?

South should balance with 1NT which he can make. However, West may continue with 2♣. If so, he will strike gold as this is his place to play. A proper balance was made and you win some and you lose some. Take special note that if NS play the hand, South should declare in order to have his cards maintain their value. The lead will come "up" to him rather than "through" him if by some chance, North should declare.

#293.

North
♠A7643
♥94
♦QT
♣K864

West	East
♠KJ	♠T52
♥AQT82	♥65
♦J9	♦K7542
♣AT97	♣532

South
♠Q98
♥KJ73
♦A863
♣QJ

West Deals:

W	N	E	S
1♥	P	P	?

Once again the 1♥ opening is passed to South for a 1NT balance. Regardless of whether West passes or bids 2♣, North will bid 2♠, secure in the knowledge that his chances of making the contract are outstanding opposite South's action. He certainly hopes that East or West will try to compete to 3♣ so he can double for penalties. As Captain, North is in the catbird's seat. With a little more strength, he would bid game in spades. Knowing partner will *balance*, North easily passes rather than try a risky and shaky overcall after the opening bid.

#294.

North
♠AQ5
♥J973
♦KQJ
♣JT5

West
♠43
♥AQT82
♦96
♣AK98

East
♠JT976
♥54
♦8432
♣43

South
♠K82
♥K6
♦AT75
♣Q762

West Deals:

W	N	E	S
1♥	P	P	?

In all four examples, West's opening hand is almost identical. Each of South's balancing hands have about the same strength with varied shape. North, as Captain, has had his share and not much more. In this instance, he has far more than his "fair share" but has no immediate bid. He acts accordingly by bidding game in NT after the balancing bid. It must be strongly emphasized that in the second seat, action does **NOT** have to be taken because of a "fear" that partner will sell out to the opponents. Too many players act immediately with the North hand.

Balancing After an Opening Suit-Bid and a Response

Very often, a balancing opportunity is presented when an opponent opens the bidding, a response is made and the auction quickly ceases. Once there has been a response, the Opener's hand is usually "limited" after he makes his rebid, especially if he passes.

Great emphasis is placed on the fact that the opening bidder's rebid is a very important bid in bridge. Knowledge of this fact is paramount when considering whether to balance. Several auctions follow in which West opens the bidding and his partner responds. In each bidding sequence the Opener and his partner decide to quit the bidding arena early. This offers the opponents an opportunity to balance. Each of Opener's rebids in a suit tend to show "true" minimum hands of 13–15 points including distribution.

No-trump rebids always indicate high-card points. However, there are many hands with which Opener would make a minimum rebid when in fact he may have a minimum-plus hand.

In this area of bidding and analysis, it is imperative that some minimum auctions be shown and studied. Possible balancing action might be taken in the following sequences. Study each auction and then read the comments which follow. **YOU** are in the dead seat! Of course, your action depends on your cards. The concept being developed is to learn to recognize when a balancing action might *be appropriate*.

#295.

(a)					(b)			
W	N	E	S		W	N	E	S
1♣	P	1♥	P		1♦	P	1♥	P
1♠	P	P	??		2♣	P	P	??

(a) West has clubs and spades. East has hearts and three or four spades. If he has four, he would have raised partner with 8-10 points. If he has three, he would have bid 1NT with 8-10 H.C. points, no singleton, and a diamond stopper. Both sides have strength but the opponents have the ranking suits. South may have a good enough hand with which to balance, but such an action should be discouraged.

(b) West has diamonds and clubs, but not four spades. East has hearts and a club preference. Both sides have strength, but N–S tend to have the ranking suit. Study your hand carefully and picture partner's possible shape. Probable balance.

♥ ♠ ♣ ♦

(c)			
W	N	E	S
1♦	P	1♥	P
2♦	P	P	??

(d)			
W	N	E	S
1♥	P	1♠	P
2♦	P	P	??

(c) West has diamonds but NOT four hearts or four spades. He also doesn't rate to have four clubs. With a reasonably balanced hand and stoppers, he would have rebid 1NT. East has hearts and maybe four spades but not much strength. Tend to balance.

(d) West has hearts and diamonds and East has spades and a diamond preference so you should have an idea how many hearts are in partner's hand. N–S, among their other cards, should have clubs but would have to bid at the three-level. Shy away from balancing in the minors against the majors, especially in the danger zone.

(e)			
W	N	E	S
1♦	P	1♠	P
2♦	P	P	??

(f)			
W	N	E	S
1♦	P	1♥	P
1NT	P	P	??

(e) West doesn't have four spades and probably doesn't have four clubs. He also failed to rebid 1NT. This sequence and your analysis may lead to a balance.

(f) West doesn't have either four hearts OR four spades. He probably has some type of balanced distribution for NT play. Nevertheless, a balancing action is often in order.

(g)

W	N	E	S
1♣	P	1♠	P
2♠	P	P	??

(h)

W	N	E	S
1♣	P	1♦	P
2♦	P	P	??

(g) West has spades and a definite fit in the master suit. Unless you have great distribution and a very long red suit, don't even try a balance.

(h) West is often six–four in clubs and diamonds. If he were five–five or five–four, or occasionally four–five, he might have opened 1♦ intending to rebid 2♣. N–S has a major-suit fit, maybe two of them. This auction demands a balance.

(i)

W	N	E	S
1♥	P	2♥	P
P	??		

(j)

W	N	E	S
1♥	P	1♠	P
2♥	P	P	??

(i) In this auction, E-W have a guaranteed eight-card fit or longer. When this occurs, the opponents <u>also have a fit.</u> The chances are very good for a successful balance.

(j) Stay away from this one. The opponents have both master suits and you would have to act at the three-level. A balance here would work occasionally but the percentage for success is poor.

(k)

W	N	E	S
1♣	P	1♦	P
2♣	P	2♦	P
P	??		

(l)

W	N	E	S
1♣	P	1♦	P
1♥	P	1NT	P
P	??		

(k) West doesn't have four hearts or four spades. He is long in clubs and East is long in diamonds. A fit exists for N-S at the two-level or higher.

(l) Although East doesn't have four spades, West could. It is difficult (but not impossible) to barge into an auction such as this. It is most likely that whoever plays the hand will fail.

VERY IMPORTANT: The reader should have gleaned, from <u>many</u> of the examples, a sense of treading on "thin ice." When sitting in the re-opening seat and looking at your cards, the balancing actions aren't always obvious. It is the *auction* that makes it obvious and you must fit your cards into it. No one questions the sensitivity of executing a "balance," but it is hoped that you see the tremendous importance it has in the bidding structure. Your ability to re-open the bidding correctly when you should will determine whether your partner will learn to pass many hands that he <u>should</u> pass rather than taking premature bids that often lead to poor results.

DON'T FORGET: Generally, (1) tend to balance to get into a suit when "short" in the bidder's suit on your left; (2) always be alert to the location of the spade suit when balancing; (3) rarely balance when you have to enter the three-level; (4) be alert to the rhythm of the bidding and be aware of the opponents' bidding mannerisms.

Bidding in Response to a Balance

If you concluded that balancing is a sensitive part of bridge to master, you might feel it was "duck soup" compared to the conceptual approach of responding after your partner has re-opened the bidding for you. There is no question that your action will largely depend on your ability to determine *where* the high-cards lay and *what* is a likely distribution for that particular hand. It is an exercise in the basic bridge lessons of **SIZE** and **SHAPE**. If one assumes that he has a well-educated idea of strength and distribution, he then makes his decision whether to bid or pass based on his determination of **WINNERS** and **LOSERS!**

Following are three hands which were _passed_ by SOUTH after an opening bid on his right. These hands and the paragraph which immediately follows them are re-printed from the third page of this subject. The opening bid is shown as well as South's hand, and the auction will continue to a point where his partner, sitting NORTH, "balances." Different _balancing actions_ as reflected by the ?? will be discussed and the thoughts and possible _re-actions_ by South will be considered in the explanations as the text continues. (See examples on pages 228–233.)

(a)		(b)		(c)	
East	South	East	South	East	South
1♥	♠62	1♠	♠K982	1♣	♠4
	♥J9642		♥A653		♥K532
	◆AKQ		◆KT73		◆AKJ8
	♣K72		♣A		♣AQ97

E	S	W	N	E	S	W	N	E	S	W	N
1♥	P	P	??	1♠	P	P	??	1♣	P	P	??

Note that in each of the hands, South holds cards in the opponent's bid suit. A true trap! In addition to this phenomenon of holding cards in the opponent's suit, one will often hold other hands which are good in value but poor in shape. It is best to pass under this circumstance, also. This pass is a type of trap. Taking an imperfect bidding action on hands such as these would be terribly misleading to partner.

◆ ♠ ♥ ♣

With hand (a)...

If North balances with **1♠**, he cannot have a good hand and may have only a four-card suit. Remember, North is bidding with less than would be expected if he were in the "overcall" seat. N–S has little or no chance for game. If East passes after the balance, South should probably "pass" but might consider a "one no-trump" bid. If East bids 2♥, South should "double" for penalties, planning on winning three diamond tricks, two heart tricks, and either his club King or a trick from partner—maybe both.

If North balances with a **DOUBLE**, he promises 10 or 11 high-card points as his minimum. South should incorporate the score into his thinking. If the vulnerability is either even or favorable, he should think "pass." Even if partner has the barest minimum of 10 points, declarer may be defeated as much as three tricks. N–S may have a game in no-trump but so what? If the game is there, imagine the beating E-W will take if they play it. If N-S are vulnerable against non-vulnerable opponents, a "2NT" bid (which shows this hand) might be best. North will bid game if he has opening-bid values for his double.

If North balances with a jump to **2♠** or **3♣**, he promises the values for a double and it's easy to determine both his shape and his high-card placement. Bid "3NT" and you'll make it.

If North balances with **1NT**, he promises 11 points or more in high-cards. South should bid "3NT". The contract will make a high percentage of the time. North has something in hearts and can continually work on the opening bidder.

With hand (b)...

If North balances with **2♣**, he has good values, but a deficiency in heart length or he would have doubled. The prospects of game are extremely remote. "Pass."

If North balances with 2♥, your hand is tremendous regardless of what partner has in overall strength. You know he is short in spades so with almost any holding, he should be able to play for three losers. Bid "4♥."

If North balances with a **DOUBLE**, game is assured and slam is possible if North has the right cards. Could North have a singleton or doubleton spade, four or five hearts to the K Q and the A Q or A J of diamonds? He could, so South must make a forcing bid to elicit more information. How about a powerful cue-bid of "2♠"? If partner bids 3♥, raise him to game and if he jumps in hearts in response to the "cue," check out the aces and try for the slam.

If North balances with a **JUMP IN A SUIT**, game should be bid. If he jumps in hearts, bid the "heart game" and maybe try for a slam. If he jumps in diamonds or clubs, bid **3NT!**

If North balances with 1NT, just bid "3NT." Don't use Stayman to look for the major suit (hearts) fit. If it exists, the fact that partner balanced with 1NT shows that he has cards (how about QJx) in the opponent's suit. This indicates that Opener's partner is singleton or void in spades and he will be able to "ruff" spade leads to defeat 4♥ provided Opener has the Ace to lead!

♥ ♠ ♦ ♣

With hand (c)...

If North balances with 1♠, just pass. Game is out of the question and he will need everything you have in order to make the contract. However, if he balances with either 1♦ or 1♥, a cue-bid is mandatory to show great strength and to try for game.

If North balances with a **DOUBLE**, vulnerability will influence your action. If it is favorable, a penalty pass is mandatory. If it isn't, then a cue-bid should be made to show power and to seek a possible heart fit. Without a heart fit, 3NT will be the final contract.

If North balances with a **JUMP IN A SUIT**, game is assured if his bid is spades and a very possible slam exists if his bid is diamonds or hearts. The fact that a full opening bid can be held by East should *not* preclude slam possibilities by North–South.

If North balances with **1NT**, use Stayman to try for the major suit (hearts) fit. If it exists, bid the heart game because you hold the first-round control of Opener's club suit unlike the example given in hand (b). If not, then bid 3NT.

The basic presentation on **BALANCING** is complete. There are very few adjuncts to the material. A handful of tournament players using a highly sophisticated system may add a few wrinkles here and there, but everything you need to know has been covered. Perhaps the two most important thoughts which will guide and assist you regarding the concept of "balancing" are (1) learn to pass in the immediate seat rather than overcall or double with skimpy values—this leads to "balancing"; and (2) develop (through practice) sound judgment regarding when to balance and which balancing action to take.

IMPORTANT note regarding the Stayman convention!! After partner makes a balancing bid of 1NT, Responder may wish to look for a "major-suit fit." To activate the Stayman convention, a cue-bid of the opening bidder's suit is the preferred method.

SUMMATION

1. Overcall and/or double with decent values which will encourage you to...

2. Pass when a sound overcall or double doesn't exist which **may** lead to...

3. A *balancing* action by partner which can be...

4. A suit-bid which is usually quite weak or...

5. A double which may be weaker than normally expected or...

6. A jump bid which is a decent hand but less than normally expected or...

7. A no-trump bid which is less than a normal no-trump overcall.

When partner *balances*, consider the size and shape needed for his action and remember that he knows you have cards and he has already bid some of **your values**. Any time you bid in response to a *balance* you will be showing a good hand. Don't go crazy as you...

8. Try to estimate your winners and/or losers so you can...

9. Determine whether to raise, try for game, bid a game, try for slam, penalize the opponents or start looking for a new partner.

You have now been exposed to the true backbone of standard bidding methods which have been time-tested and proven to be sound. Yes, there are variations, some of which are used by your best friends. However, if you learn this material, you are well on your way to becoming a good Bridge player.

It is expected that while learning to bid, you were also practicing elementary play. You must remember that if you and your partner *cannot* reach the proper contracts, superior play will not bail you out of bad scores.

BID to the correct contract and KNOW your partner's hand!

CONCLUSION

This book is now finished and it is my fervent wish that the material you read has been assimilated properly. It is a conceptual approach to basics predicated on reason and logic. Its elements can be a rock-solid foundation upon which to build any good partnership. Furthermore, it is easy to construct viable alternatives in method to enhance the ones presented on these pages.

For instance, many modern tournament players of today do not recognize all of opener's reverse bidding as powerful hands in the true standard structure. Standard bidding says that an unforced rebid by Opener at the level of two or more in a higher ranking suit than that bid originally is a strength-showing bid. Two examples of standard reverses are:

#1. 1♣ — Pass — 1♥ or 1♠ — Pass
     2♦

#2. 1♣ — Pass — 1♠ — Pass
     2♥

Some players play a system called "Two Over One forcing to game" so, within their structure, the sequence of

$$1\heartsuit — Pass — 2\clubsuit — Pass$$
$$2\spadesuit$$

shows no more than a minimum hand for opener. This is because the two-level response created a game force. However, using their method in which a reverse shows no added values, other problems are created when Opener "reverses" with a minimum and Responder also has minimum values. There is a tendency for partnerships to wander into an unsound game when both players have minimum values.

Regardless of what system you now play or might play in the future, what this book has offered you is the information and opportunity to develop a keen, sound, and disciplined game. It is absolutely certain that if you master this fundamental approach, you will soon be playing at a level which puts you in the top five percent of the players in the nation.